THE NATIONAL CONSUMER LAW CENTER

SURVIVING CREDIT CARD DEBT WORKBOOK

FOR CONSUMERS AND THEIR ADVOCATES

WITH CD ROM

AUTHOR

DEANNE LOONIN

NATIONAL CONSUMER LAW CENTER
77 Summer St., 10th Floor
Boston, MA 02110-1006
(617) 542-8010
www.consumerlaw.org

Acknowledgments

This workbook was made possible through support from the following: Attorneys General Consumer Protection and Education Fund, National Conference for Bankruptcy Judges Endowment for Education and Administration on Aging, Department of Health and Human Services, (Grant number 90-AP-2640). Points of view are entirely those of the National Consumer Law Center.

The author would like to thank Carolyn Carter and John Rao for their substantive contributions and extensive editing assistance and Neil Fogarty, Lightbourne, Shannon Halbrook, Jon Sheldon, and Donna Wong for production assistance.

About NCLC

The National Consumer Law Center, a non-profit corporation founded in 1969 and dedicated to the interests of low-income consumers, provides technical support and consulting services to legal services attorneys, government agencies, and private attorneys representing consumers. See our web site for more information at www.consumerlaw.org.

Training

NCLC conducts national, regional and local consumer law trainings. We also hold annual conferences on consumer rights litigation and other issues.

Case Consulting

Case analysis and consulting for lawyers representing low-income consumers are among NCLC's primary activities. Administration on Aging funding allows us to provide free consulting to advocates representing elderly consumers on many types of cases.

Ordering Publications

Publications Department, National Consumer Law Center, 77 Summer St., 10th Floor, Boston, MA 02110-1006, (617) 542-9595; Fax (617) 542-8028; Email: publications@nclc.org.

Attention

This publication is designed to provide authoritative information concerning the subject matter covered. Always use other sources for more recent developments or for special rules for individual jurisdictions. This publication cannot substitute for the independent judgment and skills of an attorney or other professional. Nonattorneys are cautioned against using these materials to conduct a lawsuit without advice from an attorney and are cautioned against engaging in the unauthorized practice of law.

Copyright

ISBN 1-931697-69-8
Library of Congress Control Number: 2005923305

Cover and interior design: Lightbourne, Inc., www.lightbourne.com
Cover photography: www.Gettyimages.com

CONTENTS

CD-Rom Contents

Forms, Checklists and Sample Letters from This Workbook

Consumer Education Information

Advocate's Materials

Sample Pleadings

SECTION ONE:

First Steps

 **CHAPTER 1: Introduction**

 **CHAPTER 2: Are You in Trouble?**

 **CHAPTER 3: Budgeting Tips**

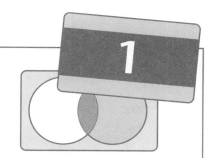

Introduction

If You Have Credit Card Debt, You are Not Alone

Consumer credit card debt in the United States almost tripled between 1989 and 2001. Savings rates have gone down and the number of consumers filing for personal bankruptcy has soared. There are many explanations for these trends, including increases in housing and health care costs and declines in real income. For many families in the United States, credit cards fill the growing gap between household income and basic living expenses.

Creditors also deserve much of the blame for the explosion in credit card debt. Changes in laws and court decisions over the past few decades have greatly benefited creditors. Creditors are more aggressive than ever in marketing credit cards, even to consumers with shaky credit histories. Creditors also continue to come up with ways to charge new types of fees and make greater profits. Late fees and other penalties make it nearly impossible for consumers to dig themselves out of trouble once they start getting behind on their credit card payments.

CREDIT CARD DEBT: It's Happening to Everyone

Are you over 65 and in credit card debt? If so, you're not alone.

The average self-reported credit card debt among seniors over age 65 increased by 89% between 1992 and 2001, to $4,041.[1] During that same time period, seniors between 65 and 69 saw the most staggering rise in credit card debt—217%. Bankruptcy filings are higher than ever among seniors as well.

Are you in the middle class and in credit card debt? If so, you're not alone.

Credit debt among middle class families grew by 75% between 1989 and 2001.[2]

Are you in the lower income class and in credit card debt? If so, you're not alone.

Credit card debt among very low-income families grew by 184% between 1989 and 2001.[3]

Are you a college student and in credit card debt? If so, you're not alone.

In 2001, 83% of all undergraduate students had credit cards. This percentage jumped to 96% for college seniors. For all undergraduates, the average number of credit cards was 4.25. Seniors averaged just over six credit cards each.[4]

---

1. Tamara Draut and Heather C. McGhee, *Retiring in the Red: The Growth of Debt Among Older Americans* (Demos, February 2004).
2. Tamara Draut and Javier Silva, *Borrowing to Make Ends Meet: The Growth of Credit Card Debt in the '90s* (Demos, September 2003). These figures may be substantially underreported. The figures are based on data that consumers reported about themselves in surveys.
3. Id.
4. Nellie Mae, *Undergraduate Students and Credit Cards: An Analysis of Usage Rates and Trends* (April 2002).

Everyone has financial problems at one time or another. You are not alone if you are experiencing these problems. You are also not alone if you continue to feel embarrassed, humiliated or panicked about your situation. These feelings are common and can cause a lot of stress for you and your family.

This pressure can cause quarrels, temporary separations, or even divorce. Mental health counseling, family therapy, and marriage counseling may be useful for managing the stress of financial problems. If you have health insurance, your policy may include free or low-cost mental health assistance. It can't hurt to ask your doctor. This type of assistance is also usually available from a variety of organizations on a sliding-scale fee basis or for free. Call a trusted local credit counseling agency or family services for a reference. You can also call and ask a therapist about low-cost or free mental health counseling options available in the community.

Whatever course you choose, it is important that you remain aware of the additional stress you may be feeling and that you try to deal with it in the healthiest possible way.

USING THIS WORKBOOK

Access to affordable credit is essential for many people and not everyone who carries credit card debt is in trouble. Many people are able to make their credit card payments on time and pay off their debts. Many are able to pay their balances every month. This workbook may still be helpful if you are one of those people, but it is mainly intended for consumers who are in trouble.

The focus of this handbook is credit card debt. If you are having problems with other types of debt, such as home or car loans, you should seek legal assistance as soon as possible. These types of secured debts are almost always going to be your highest priorities. If you can't pay those debts, you are in danger of losing the roof over your head or your wheels to get to work.

There are many resources available to help people with debt problems. Many of these resources are listed in the bibliography. This workbook will not repeat everything that can be found in these other resources. Instead, it will focus on helping consumers and their advocates understand whether they are in trouble and learn about important strategies to get out of trouble.

The main strategies covered are:
- Using Current Income or Raising Money to Pay Off Debts (Chapters 4 and 5);
- Negotiating With Creditors (Chapter 6);
- Finding Help from A Credit Counseling Agency (Chapter 7); and
- Bankruptcy (Chapter 9).

We also briefly discuss strategies that are likely to get you into even more trouble, including:

- Taking Out Unaffordable or Predatory Loans (Chapter 5);
- "Debt Settlement" Companies (Chapter 8);
- Fraudulent Debt Elimination or Debt Termination Companies (Chapter 8); and
- Credit Repair Companies. (Chapter 8).

The first section of the workbook is geared toward both consumers and their advocates. The second section is intended mainly for advocates. The advocate's section includes information about legal challenges against deceptive credit counseling and debt settlement companies. It also includes detailed information about critical consumer protection laws that apply to consumers with debt problems.

All of the forms in both sections are also included on the companion CD-Rom. We encourage you to make copies of the forms in the book or print out blank forms from the CD. The CD also contains sample pleadings for advocates as well as summaries of relevant laws and consumer education information. Instructions for using the CD-Rom can be found at the back of the book.

We encourage you to refer to the glossary whenever you see a term you aren't sure about. The bibliography includes a list of additional resources, web sites and information on how to find legal assistance.

Are You In Trouble?

Whether you are in over your head in debt depends a lot on your individual circumstances. However, there are general warning signs that apply in most situations. These warning signs of credit card trouble include:

✓ CHECKLIST CHECK ALL THAT APPLY:

❑ You are only paying the minimum amounts required on your credit card accounts, or maybe even less. **Note: This may be OK every now and then, but if you are regularly making just the minimum payment, it is a warning sign.**

❑ You are consistently paying your credit card bills late.

❑ The outstanding balance on your credit cards is growing and hardly ever decreases.

❑ You have more credit cards than you can keep track of.

❑ You are at or very close to the limit on each of your credit cards.

❑ You frequently are applying for new cards to transfer balances from old cards.

❑ You're playing the credit card game by signing up for every credit card that sends you an unsolicited offer.

❑ You have received phone calls or letters about delinquent credit card bill payments.

❑ You are using your credit card to buy necessities like food or gas, but you can't pay the monthly balances.

❑ Your credit cards are no longer used for the sake of convenience, but because you don't have money.

❑ You are dipping into savings or your I.R.A. to pay your monthly bills.

❑ You are going to very high rate lenders such as payday lenders to help you meet your monthly expenses, including credit card bills.

❑ You've taken out the maximum cash advance on at least one card.

❑ You have just lost your job or are facing a family emergency or disability and are concerned about how you will pay all your bills.[5]

How many boxes did you check?   TOTAL _____

If you checked more than two or three items, you are probably in trouble or on the way to trouble.

5. Some of the items on this list were excerpted from Jenny C. McCune, "In a Credit Crunch? You May Need Professional Help," bankrate.com (February 26, 2002).

There are different levels of financial problems. For example, you may be just starting to experience problems. In that case, you should tighten your budget and figure out whether you can get a better deal with the credit cards you now hold or shop around for more favorable terms. Tips about prevention and shopping for the right card are included on the companion CD-Rom.

Or, you might be facing a temporary bump in the road. Maybe you've lost your job but are likely to find another one soon. In that case, there are some temporary solutions that might work for you, but not for someone who is facing longer term problems.

Even if you feel that you're OK, the advice in this workbook may help you deal with potential problems before you're in trouble. You may even want to talk to a credit counselor or other adviser to help you at this early stage. This can be a good idea as long as you know that you're going to the counselor for a very limited purpose—to get advice on budgeting and help prevent digging a deeper financial hole. As you will see, it is easy to get roped in by credit counselors that are trying to make money off of you. Be careful, but don't be scared if you feel that some professional advice would help. Tips on choosing credit counselors are included in Chapter 7.

ORDERING YOUR CREDIT REPORT

Another good way to find out more about your situation is to order your credit report. Although you may not want to see how bad the report looks, it's best to know what you're up against.

Because there can be differences in the reports kept by each of the three major national credit bureaus, you should get your report from all three. Contact information for the three national bureaus, Experian, TransUnion and Equifax, is listed below.

You can get your report for free once a year if you live in Colorado, Georgia, Maryland, Massachusetts, New Jersey, or Vermont. These states have laws that give consumers in their states special rights. By September 2005, everyone in the country will have similar rights, as discussed below.

Regardless of where you live, credit bureaus are also required to give you a copy of your report for free if you have been denied credit within the past sixty days. You can also get one free report in any twelve-month period if you:

- Are unemployed and will be applying for a job within the next sixty days;
- Are receiving public welfare assistance; or
- Have reason to believe that the file at the credit bureau contains inaccurate information due to fraud.

In addition, credit bureaus must provide you with a free report if you have requested a fraud alert.

In addition to the separate rights to free credit reports discussed above, by September 2005, all consumers will be able to get one free credit report from each of the three major credit reporting bureaus each year. The free credit reports will become available on a rolling basis, starting with consumers living on the west coast and finishing with those on the east.

To get the report for free, go to www.annualcreditreport.com. You can find out more from the Federal Trade Commission's web site at www.ftc.gov or call the FTC's Consumer Response Center at 1-877-382-4357. You can also order free reports directly from the credit bureaus, but if you do this, be careful not to sign up for credit monitoring services that you don't want. You can order reports from all three major credit bureaus at the same time or stagger your requests over the course of the year.

If you are not entitled to a free report, you can order your report from the credit bureaus, either online, in writing, or by calling a toll-free telephone number. Each of the three major bureaus also offers a package that allows you to get all three reports at once. Each company requires you to give certain information to order a report and each has a toll-free number that you can call for more information. The current toll-free phone numbers and web addresses for ordering credit reports are listed below. You can also order by mail, but these addresses change frequently and it is best to call or e-mail to get the current mail address.

- Experian's toll-free telephone number to order reports is 1-888-EXPERIAN (1-888-397-3742), TTY (1-800-972-0322). You can also order on-line at www.experian.com.
- Equifax's number is 1-800-685-1111. Reports can also be ordered on-line at www.equifax.com.
- TransUnion Corporation's phone number is 1-800-888-4213. Reports can be ordered on-line at www.tuc.com.

Credit bureaus can charge you no more than $9.50 per report. You should note that Congress periodically increases this limit.

Budgeting Tips

A budget or spending plan is a list of the income and expenses you expect each month. The best way to come up with your actual monthly budget is to keep track for a few months and write down your expenses and income.

This can be a much less formal process than it sounds. The forms provided in this chapter are helpful for some people, but you do not need to use them if you would rather come up with your own way of making a budget. Regardless of how you get there, the main goal is for you to get an understanding of how much money you and your family bring in each month and how much you spend. It is important to write this information down in a way that you can follow and keep track of.

The first step is to make an initial budget. The instructions below will help you do this. The next step is to keep track of your income and expenses for a few months to see if your budget is accurate. Before going through the information below, you should collect resources that will help you such as your paycheck stubs to review your income and your checking account log or credit card records to get a sense of your expenses.

YOUR INITIAL BUDGET

Start by writing down your current income and expenses. Separate forms to track income and expenses are printed below. You can use these forms if you're comfortable with them or make up your own.

INCOME

For the income budget, include all sources of income that you and others in your household receive on a regular basis, including wages, child support, or public assistance. Only include income that you reasonably expect to get each month. If you know of an expected change and that change is certain, you can use it in planning your budget. If the change is very unlikely, it's best not to include it in your budget plan.

EXPENSES

The expense form below lists common expenses. You should also write down any of your expenses that are not on the list.

For expenses that may not occur every month, try to think of how much you spend each year and divide that amount by twelve. For example, if you spend about $400/year on clothes for your family, this will come out to almost $34/month.

The expense sheet has a separate section for credit cards and other past due bills. These spaces are for payments you are making to pay back previously owed charges. When you start writing down your current budget, new credit card charges should be listed in the appropriate "expense" category.

For example, you may have a balance of $5,000 on your Visa card. If you pay $100 each month to try to pay this down, you should list this amount in the credit card section. If you use your Visa to buy $200 worth of groceries, this amount should be listed in the food category. This will help you see how you are using your credit cards.

The income and expense forms for your initial budget are printed below. You will find additional forms at the end of this chapter and on the CD Rom that should be used to help you keep track of your income and expenses for the next few months.

BUDGETING FORMS: Keeping Track of Income

INITIAL MONTHLY INCOME BUDGET

MONTH _____ YEAR _____

SOURCE OF INCOME	YOU	SPOUSE, PARTNER, OR OTHER CONTRIBUTING HOUSEHOLD MEMBER	TOTAL
Employment			
Overtime			
Child Support/Alimony			
Pension			
Interest Income			
Public Benefits			
Dividends			
Trust Payments			
Royalties			
Rents Received			
Help from Friends or Relatives			
Other Income			
TOTAL			

INITIAL MONTHLY EXPENSE BUDGET

(Combine for you, your spouse, partner or other joint debtor)

MONTH _____ YEAR _____

Home Related Expenses

Mortgage or Rent _____

Second Mortgage _____

Third Mortgage _____

Real Estate Taxes _____

Insurance _____

Condo Fees _____

Mobile Home Lot Rent _____

Home Maintenance/Upkeep _____

Other _____

Utilities

Gas _____

Electric _____

Oil _____

Water/Sewer _____

Telephone _____

Land Line _____

Cell _____

Cable T.V. _____

Internet Connection
or Service _____

Other _____

Medical

Current Needs _____

Prescriptions _____

Dental _____

Insurance Co-Payments
or Other Premiums _____

Other _____

Food

Groceries _____

Eating Out _____

Transportation

Car Payments _____

Car Insurance _____

Gas _____

Car Maintenance _____

Public Transportation _____

Miscellaneous

Clothing _____

Laundry and Cleaning _____

Life Insurance Premiums _____

Alimony or Support Paid _____

Student Loan Payments _____

Entertainment _____

Newspapers/Magazines _____

Pet Expenses _____

Tuition for Children's School _____

Religious Expenses _____

Amounts Owed on Debts

Credit Card _____

Credit Card _____

Credit Card _____

Medical Bill _____

Medical Bill _____

Other _____

Cosigned Debts _____

Other Expenses _____

TOTAL EXPENSES _____

TOTALS

You should then subtract your expenses from your income. Write those amounts here:

INITIAL BUDGET

MONTH _____ **YEAR** _____

INCOME _____ − **EXPENSES** _____ = _____

You should not be surprised if you find out that your expenses exceed your income.
This is why you are having financial problems.

ADJUSTING YOUR INITIAL BUDGET

Once you have come up with a budget, you should try to live with it for a month or so to get a sense of whether it correctly reflects your actual income and expenses. Once you've kept track for a few months, ask yourself if you have any extra money left over to put toward your debts. Regardless, we suggest that you try to figure out ways to tighten your budget.

The first question is whether you can make helpful changes to your budget by either reducing expenses, increasing income, or, in the best case scenario, doing both. There are many books and guides that can help you with both the income and expense sides of your budget. The list below includes a few of these resources. A more complete list can be found in the bibliography.

Selected Budgeting Resources:

> National Consumer Law Center, *Guide to Surviving Debt* (2005 Edition). See www.nclc.org.
> Michelle Singletary, *Seven Money Mantras for a Richer Life* (Random House, 2004)
> Robin Leonard, *Money Troubles* (Nolo, 9th ed. 2003). See www.nolo.com.
> Federal Trade Commission, *FTC Facts for Consumers, Knee-Deep in Debt.* See www.ftc.gov.
> Consumer Literacy Consortium, *66 Ways to Save Money*, available on-line at www.pueblo.gsa.gov.

The main goal is to come up with realistic options such as working overtime to bring in more income or cutting back on restaurant meals to decrease expenses.

You will find a lot of advice, including some of the resources listed above, about how to cut expenses. Much of this advice is helpful, but not every idea will work for everyone. As you consider cutting your expenses, it is important, above all, that you understand what your choices are, how you could change your spending habits, and the consequences of your decisions. You should also understand that this is not going to be easy. Cutting expenses is hard work and takes a lot of commitment. Try to work together with your family to understand the situation and to figure out ways to make it better. As part of this commitment, you will need to think about putting away your credit cards, at least for a while. Consider keeping only one to use for emergencies.

Try to be realistic while also making a serious commitment to cut expenses. A few examples:

1. Many budget books will tell you to save money by spending less during the winter holidays. Nobody is suggesting that you buy no gifts at all. The point is to understand how much you spend and to see if you can save money by spending less. For example, can you work out an agreement with your relatives that you will only buy gifts for the children, not for the adults, or that you will all limit the amount you spend on gifts to a certain amount?

2. Food is another good example. You probably don't realize how much you spend on food. When you add up your monthly food costs, be sure and count not only purchases at grocery stores, but also eating out.

You can save money on food in all kinds of ways, including:

- Using coupons to save money on products you would generally buy.
- Shopping at different stores to get the best prices.
- Planning menus ahead of time instead of at the grocery store.
- Trying not to shop when you're hungry!
- Shopping without your kids if possible.
- Buying the cheaper store brands.
- Eating at home whenever possible.
- Packing a lunch for school or work rather than eating out.
- Bringing coffee to work or drinking free coffee at your office if it's available.[6]

6. Excerpted in part from Dahlstrom and Co. with contributions from Consumer Credit Counseling Service of Greater Dallas, *Money Sense, Credit Wise: What You Don't Owe Can't Hurt You* (2003).

STOP TELEMARKETING CALLS

You can save money by not buying products from telemarketers or signing up for sweepstakes or lotteries with these companies. To avoid being tempted by telemarketers, sign up for the Federal Trade Commission's "do-not-call" list. You may register online at www.donotcall.gov or by phone by calling 1-888-382-1222 (TTY 1-866-290-4236). You must call from the telephone number you wish to register. Registration with the FTC's do-not-call registry is free. If you register online you must provide an email address for confirmation. Once you have registered, your telephone number will remain on the registry for five years, or until it is disconnected or you delete it from the registry. After five years you can renew your registration. Your state may also maintain a "do-not-call" list. You can contact your state attorney general or state consumer protection program to learn if your state has such a list and how it may protect you.

BUDGETING FORMS: Keeping Track of Income

MONTHLY INCOME BUDGET

MONTH _____   YEAR _____

SOURCE OF INCOME	YOU	SPOUSE, PARTNER, OR OTHER CONTRIBUTING HOUSEHOLD MEMBER	TOTAL
Employment			
Overtime			
Child Support/Alimony			
Pension			
Interest Income			
Public Benefits			
Dividends			
Trust Payments			
Royalties			
Rents Received			
Help from Friends or Relatives			
Other Income			
TOTAL			

MONTHLY EXPENSE BUDGET

(Combine for you, your spouse, partner or other joint debtor)

MONTH _____   YEAR _____

Home Related Expenses

Mortgage or Rent _____

Second Mortgage _____

Third Mortgage _____

Real Estate Taxes _____

Insurance _____

Condo Fees _____

Mobile Home Lot Rent _____

Home Maintenance/Upkeep _____

Other _____

Utilities

Gas _____

Electric _____

Oil _____

Water/Sewer _____

Telephone _____

Land Line _____

Cell _____

Cable T.V. _____

Internet Connection
or Service _____

Other _____

Medical

Current Needs _____

Prescriptions _____

Dental _____

Insurance Co-Payments
or Other Premiums _____

Other _____

Food

Groceries _____

Eating Out _____

Transportation

Car Payments _____

Car Insurance _____

Gas _____

Car Maintenance _____

Public Transportation _____

Miscellaneous

Clothing _____

Laundry and Cleaning _____

Life Insurance Premiums _____

Alimony or Support Paid _____

Student Loan Payments _____

Entertainment _____

Newspapers/Magazines _____

Pet Expenses _____

Tuition for Children's School _____

Religious Expenses _____

Amounts Owed on Debts

Credit Card _____

Credit Card _____

Credit Card _____

Medical Bill _____

Medical Bill _____

Other _____

Cosigned Debts _____

Other Expenses _____

TOTAL EXPENSES _____

BUDGETING FORMS: Keeping Track of Income

MONTHLY INCOME BUDGET

MONTH _____ YEAR _____

SOURCE OF INCOME	YOU	SPOUSE, PARTNER, OR OTHER CONTRIBUTING HOUSEHOLD MEMBER	TOTAL
Employment			
Overtime			
Child Support/Alimony			
Pension			
Interest Income			
Public Benefits			
Dividends			
Trust Payments			
Royalties			
Rents Received			
Help from Friends or Relatives			
Other Income			
TOTAL			

MONTHLY EXPENSE BUDGET

(Combine for you, your spouse, partner or other joint debtor)

MONTH _____   YEAR _____

Home Related Expenses

Mortgage or Rent _____

Second Mortgage _____

Third Mortgage _____

Real Estate Taxes _____

Insurance _____

Condo Fees _____

Mobile Home Lot Rent _____

Home Maintenance/Upkeep _____

Other _____

Utilities

Gas _____

Electric _____

Oil _____

Water/Sewer _____

Telephone _____

Land Line _____

Cell _____

Cable T.V. _____

Internet Connection
or Service _____

Other _____

Medical

Current Needs _____

Prescriptions _____

Dental _____

Insurance Co-Payments
or Other Premiums _____

Other _____

Food

Groceries _____

Eating Out _____

Transportation

Car Payments _____

Car Insurance _____

Gas _____

Car Maintenance _____

Public Transportation _____

Miscellaneous

Clothing _____

Laundry and Cleaning _____

Life Insurance Premiums _____

Alimony or Support Paid _____

Student Loan Payments _____

Entertainment _____

Newspapers/Magazines _____

Pet Expenses _____

Tuition for Children's School _____

Religious Expenses _____

Amounts Owed on Debts

Credit Card _____

Credit Card _____

Credit Card _____

Medical Bill _____

Medical Bill _____

Other _____

Cosigned Debts _____

Other Expenses _____

TOTAL EXPENSES _____

TOTALS

You should then subtract your expenses from your income. Write those amounts here:

INITIAL BUDGET

MONTH _____ YEAR _____

INCOME _____ – EXPENSES _____ = _____

FOLLOWING MONTHS

MONTH _____ YEAR _____

INCOME _____ – EXPENSES _____ = _____

MONTH _____ YEAR _____

INCOME _____ – EXPENSES _____ = _____

MONTH _____ YEAR _____

INCOME _____ – EXPENSES _____ = _____

MONTH _____ YEAR _____

INCOME _____ – EXPENSES _____ = _____

SECTION TWO:

Strategies to Deal with Debt Trouble

Can You Afford To Repay Credit Cards Using Current Income?

DO YOU OWE THE MONEY?

In order to figure out whether you can repay your credit cards, you first need to be sure that you actually owe all or part of the debt. In most cases, you will owe the money, but this is not always true. Check your monthly statements to make sure that you're only being charged for items that you bought. Did someone use your card without your permission? If so, you may be able to reduce or even eliminate the amount owed. Are there mystery charges on the credit card? The creditor may have signed you up for insurance or a club membership that you didn't want.

FAIR CREDIT AND BILLING RIGHTS

There are three separate protections for credit card consumers that find errors or experience other problems with credit card bills. Each is discussed briefly below. Consumer education handouts on these issues are included on the companion CD-Rom.

1. Unauthorized Use

Unauthorized use means that someone stole, borrowed or otherwise used your card or card number without permission. Under federal law, liability for unauthorized use of a credit card is limited to $50. You should call your creditor as soon as you know of the unauthorized use of a credit card. If you call before unauthorized charges are incurred, the lender cannot charge even $50.

If a charge unexpectedly appears on a bill for something unauthorized, you can use the billing error procedures discussed below (#2) to dispute the charge. Some credit card lenders have been telling consumers they can only report unauthorized use by sending a written billing error notice within 60 days of receiving the bill with the unauthorized charge. **This is not true.** You can report unauthorized use over the telephone. You also are not required to do so within 60 days, although the sooner, the better.

After an unauthorized charge is reported, the credit card lender must conduct a "reasonable" investigation of your claim, unless it simply decides to take the charge off of the account.

2. Billing Error Procedures

The second type of credit card protection involves disputes about a bill. These disputes may include a merchant overcharging you or charging for products that you never received. A law called the Fair Credit Billing Act forces lenders to follow specific "billing error" procedures to resolve the dispute.

You must raise a dispute within sixty (60) days of the first bill with the improper charge. The dispute must be raised **in writing** and include the following information:

- Name and account number
- The dollar amount in dispute
- A statement of the reason for the dispute

You must send letters of dispute to the address provided by the lender for this purpose. Information about this address and how to raise a dispute appears on the back of credit card statements. The law only permits consumers to raise certain types of disputes using the billing error procedures. A sample billing error dispute letter can be found below.

Credit card companies must investigate disputes and report back in writing within two complete billing cycles or within 90 days, whichever comes first. Until the dispute is resolved, you do not need to pay the disputed portion of the bill. If the credit card company does not resolve the dispute in your favor, it must send a written explanation and give any supporting documentation upon request.

SAMPLE CREDIT CARD DISPUTE LETTER

January 10, 2005

Jane Consumer
101 Main Street
Anytown, USA 12345

Big Credit Card Co.
P.O. Box 666
Somewhere, DE 11111

[The actual address you need to use appears on the back of the
credit card bill you are disputing in a section called
"Billing Rights Summary".]

Dear Big Credit Card Co.:

My name is Jane Consumer. My account number is 123456789.
I am disputing a charge on the bill you mailed on December
5, 2004. That bill includes a charge in the amount of
$2,000.00 to Fix-It Garage. This amount is in error.

In October 2004 I took my car to Fix-It Garage to be
repaired. They estimated that the work would cost $400.
I told them not to do any work in excess of $400. When
they called to say the repairs were completed, they told
me that the bill was $2,000.00. I did not agree to pay
this amount and they have charged my account without my
authorization.

I have contacted Fix-It Garage by telephone, in person,
and by the enclosed letter in order to try to resolve the
dispute. They have not agreed to withdraw the charge.

Please investigate this dispute and provide me with a
written statement of the outcome. Thank you for your time
and attention to this matter.

Very truly yours,

Jane Consumer

3. Right to Withhold Payment

The third important credit card dispute protection is the right to stop payment of any disputed amount. This is a very powerful tool that can be used when you are dissatisfied with something purchased with a credit card. You can use this power if you have a legitimate complaint about the quality of goods or services purchased with the card **and** you first make a good faith effort to resolve the problem with the merchant directly.

There are a few other important limits to the stop-payment right:

- The goods or services must have cost more than $50; and
- Those goods or services must have been purchased in your home state or within 100 miles of your mailing address.

These last two limits do not apply if the credit card was issued by the seller (such as a department store card) or if the seller mailed the advertisement for the goods or services purchased. You still need to make a good faith effort to resolve the problem with the seller in these circumstances. More information about credit card rights can be found on the CD-Rom and in the National Consumer Law Center publications, *Guide to Surviving Debt, Consumer Banking and Payments Law,* and *Truth in Lending.*

OTHER REASONS WHY YOU MIGHT NOT OWE THE MONEY

There might be other reasons why you don't owe the credit card debt, including possible problems with the way in which the goods or services were advertised or because of illegal, unfair or deceptive debt collection conduct. If you get sued, you may want to raise these issues as defenses or counterclaims. You will likely need to consult a lawyer to find out more about defending a collection lawsuit. More information is also included in NCLC's publication *Guide to Surviving Debt.*

If you haven't been sued yet, but are facing aggressive debt collection tactics, see Chapters 10 and 11.

CHOOSING WHICH DEBTS TO PAY

Assuming that you owe the money, the next question is whether you can afford to pay it back using your current income. After reviewing the first section of this workbook, you should have a pretty good sense of your monthly budget. This alone doesn't tell you whether you should use any extra money or try to find extra money to pay off credit card debt. There are two very important additional considerations:

1. Can you pay some money towards credit card debt and pay your priority debts? This issue is discussed below.

2. What are the consequences if you end up not paying your credit card debt? This issue is discussed in Chapter 10.

Below are a few basic concepts to keep in mind when choosing which debts to pay.

Debts with collateral are top priorities. Collateral is property that a creditor has the right to take back if you do not pay a particular debt. The most common forms of collateral are your home in the case of a mortgage (or deed of trust) and your car in the case of most car loans. Creditors who have collateral are usually referred to as "secured" creditors. **These are almost always your most important creditors**.

Some other basic principles to keep in mind when making these choices are:

1. Give first priority to expenses necessary to keep food on the table and a roof over your head.

2. Pay at least the minimum required to keep essential utility service.

3. Pay car loans or leases if you need to keep your car.

4. You must pay child support debts.

5. Income tax debts and certain other tax debts are also high priority.

6. Loans without collateral, including most credit card debts, are low priority.

7. Loans with only household goods as collateral are also low priority.

8. Do not move a debt up in priority because the creditor harasses you, threatens to sue you, or threatens to ruin your credit record. Basic information about your right to challenge debt collection harassment is discussed in Chapter 11.

9. Consider fighting back when you have good legal defenses to repayment.

10. Student loans are medium priority. For more information, see National Consumer Law Center's Guide to Surviving Debt and Student Loan Law manual.

11. Cosigned debts should be treated like your other debts.

12. Refinancing is rarely the answer. It can be very expensive and it can give your creditors more opportunities to seize assets. See Chapter 5 for more information.

If you've gone through your budget and through the list above, you may have decided that you can't pay your credit cards. If this describes your situation, you might want to skip ahead to Chapter 10 which discusses the possible consequences of not paying. If after reading that chapter, you decide that the possible consequences are too great, review Chapter 3 to consider ways you might be able to tighten your budget and find extra money to pay your debts. You should also read Chapter 9 to learn more about bankruptcy.

For more information about raising money to pay your credit cards, keep reading to the next chapter. You also might want to consider getting counseling help. In that case, you should read Chapter 7 on finding a legitimate credit counselor. The counselor may come up with ideas for increasing income or reducing expenses that you did not think of on your own.

Raising Money To Pay Off Credit Cards

This chapter goes over strategies to help you raise money or use your existing assets or property to repay credit card debt. There are situations where you will need to use these strategies instead of deciding to stop payments. This is particularly true if you are likely to face serious consequences if you stop paying your credit cards. However, you should be very careful if you decide to borrow money or use assets or savings to pay off credit card debt. This chapter will help you sort out the different strategies and help you understand which are most likely to benefit you in the long run and which are most likely to get you into deeper trouble.

CHOICES TO CONSIDER, BUT WITH CAUTION

Borrowing From Friends and Relatives

Friends or relatives may be able to help you out, but be careful. In general, there is nothing wrong with accepting this help to get you through a tough period. Occasional problems arise, however, if you count on this help. Your friends and relatives may face their own financial difficulties and may withdraw their assistance—sometimes when you need it most. Debts can also cause problems between you and your friends or relatives.

Some creditors will push you to get a friend or relative to cosign with you when you are facing financial problems. You should avoid this whenever possible. The person who cosigns will be on the hook with you. Your financial problems may become theirs as well, if you cannot afford to pay. You don't want your friendships and family relationships to be on the line if your financial circumstances do not improve.

Using Your Savings

There are several things you should keep in mind about using savings or selling off assets when you are having financial problems. The most important point is that using your savings should be part of an overall plan, not your only plan. You should also think carefully about spending your retirement money. You may be tempted to dip into your retirement savings to get you through temporary financial difficulties. The most important consideration is whether you will have time to rebuild these savings before you retire. You might also consider withdrawing money from a tax-deferred account such as an I.R.A. or 401(k). There are serious disadvantages to this option, including possible tax consequences. You should seek professional advice about these options.

Despite these warnings, in some cases it might make sense for you to dip into your savings or retirement to pay essential expenses. Just be careful of falling into the trap of using your savings to finance an unrealistic lifestyle.

Selling Assets

You might consider selling a major asset such as a car or house if you can no longer afford the payments. You will almost always do better selling the property yourself rather than hoping to get cash back from a foreclosure or repossession sale. Before you do this, make sure you have alternative housing or transportation. Otherwise, you could end up in even worse trouble.

Major assets are not the only possibilities. You might be able to raise money, particularly to help you in the short term, by selling items you really don't need such as old bicycles, furniture, or other household items. You might consider a yard sale or putting an ad in a local paper.

BORROWING AGAINST YOUR HOME

Your home is your most important asset. If you have equity in your home, you may feel tempted to take out a new loan or refinance an old loan to pay off other debts. Be very careful when borrowing against the equity in your home. This is one of the riskiest steps you can take when you have financial problems. Many of these loans will hurt more than they help.

Many consolidation lenders aggressively pressure you to refinance your unsecured credit card debt into a loan secured by your home. This is almost never a good idea. By trading in unsecured debt for a mortgage loan, you face loss of your home if you continue to have financial problems.

It is almost always a bad idea to refinance unsecured debt into secured debt even if this seems to lower the interest rate you are paying. The interest rate on a mortgage loan may be lower, but mortgage loans are usually at least twenty- and more commonly thirty-year loans. Paying at a lower rate for such a long time will almost always cost you more than a higher rate on a shorter-term loan. Think of it this way: Would you ever want to pay off the pizza you bought for dinner with a credit card by stretching the payments out for thirty years? This is the result of adding your credit card debt to a mortgage loan.

You should also be wary of claims that you will get a tax advantage from a debt consolidation loan. Many lenders offering bad refinancing deals talk about the benefit of the tax deductibility of mortgage interest. Make sure you understand how your personal tax situation will be affected. For example, if you do not itemize deductions, the tax deductibility of mortgage interest is worthless.

If your home is collateral in a refinancing deal, you have the right to cancel for any reason for three business days from the date you sign the papers. Make sure you cancel in writing before the deadline. Certified mail is much safer than regular mail. The lender is required to give you a form for this purpose, but you may also cancel the loan by simply sending a signed, dated letter indicating your desire to cancel the refinancing. More information about canceling loans, including an extended right to cancel in certain circumstances, can be found in NCLC's *Guide to Surviving Debt, Stop Predatory Lending,* and *Truth in Lending* publications.

If, despite these drawbacks, you decide to consolidate your credit card debts into a loan secured by your home, seek legal advice about the particular loan you are considering. Some home equity lenders are predatory lenders who are trying to trick you into signing away your home.

SHOPPING FOR AFFORDABLE LOANS

Although you should always keep the basic principles discussed above in mind, the reality is that there may be situations where borrowing against your home makes sense. This is especially true if you believe there will be serious consequences if you do not pay your other debts.

Shopping around and finding the most affordable loan is easier said than done. In many cases, lenders use the term "alternative loans" as a secret code word for high price sub-prime or predatory loans. Although it is difficult, you should do your best to shop around. A first step is to review your credit report and credit score.

If you credit score is low (usually meaning that it is under 650 or 670), you should know that most lenders will consider you to be a riskier borrower and will probably charge you more. You should also understand that you can still shop around even if your credit score is low. Do not assume that the deal offered by a particular lender is the best you can do. Some studies have shown that up to half of all borrowers that end up with higher cost loans actually qualified for lower-cost products.

Another strategy when you shop around is to find out anything you can about the lender. If you suspect there may be problems, check with your state's attorney general, banking commission or consumer complaint hotline.

You should also review the cost estimates that lenders must give you no later than three days after applying for a loan. This is called a "good faith" estimate of settlement costs. The form the lenders use is often called a "HUD-1" form or settlement statement. Be sure and ask for this information if you don't receive it after applying for a loan. This will show the lender that you know about your rights and are taking a close look at what the lender is charging you. If you see anything that concerns you, you should seek help from a lawyer or trusted counselor.

You should examine all of the loan terms before you sign any papers. Do not look at the monthly payment as the only issue. If loan terms are not favorable, shop around for another loan. You can always walk away from signing loan papers, even at the last minute. Definitely walk away if the lender tries to change the loan terms from what you had been originally offered.

Fortunately, there are other options available in many communities where you can borrow money at reasonable rates. For example, many credit unions have various types of lending programs with more flexible criteria than most banks. There are a number of different types of community development financial institutions (CDFIs), including community development loan funds, community development credit unions, community development venture capital funds, microenterprise development loan funds and community development banks. You can find out more from the Coalition of Community Development Financial Institutions, (703) 894-0475, www.cdfi.org. You should also consider contacting the National Federation of Community Development Credit Unions, (212) 809-1850 or visit www.natfed.org.

Just as with banks, you should shop around if you are thinking of borrowing from a credit union. Do not assume that you will automatically get a better deal just because an institution has "community" in its name or seems to be friendlier or more helpful.

REVERSE MORTGAGES

Reverse mortgages are designed primarily to help seniors. In a reverse mortgage, the lender gives the homeowner cash based on the value of the property without an immediate repayment obligation. Some reverse mortgages have no repayment obligation as long as you remain in the property—no matter how long you stay. But the mortgage, including all interest and other charges, must be repaid when the last living borrower dies, sells the home, or permanently moves away.

In most reverse mortgages, the lender will look at your age (you must be at least 62 years old), the amount of equity you have in your home, and the prevailing interest rates in order to determine the amount it will lend you. In contrast to a traditional mortgage, the amount of the debt in a reverse mortgage increases over time.

Whether or not you are having financial problems, a reverse mortgage may be a good way to get some money now based on the value of your house. If you are interested, look for a bank or mortgage company in your community that offers this product.

There are pros and cons to this strategy. In general, a reverse mortgage works best for older people who have a lot of equity in their homes. You should seek reliable legal advice or financial counseling before considering this option.

Potential drawbacks include:
- The costs involved in getting a reverse mortgage can be very high.
- The amount of cash you get may not really meet your needs.
- You can borrow against your equity only once.
- A reverse mortgage can affect your eligibility to receive certain government benefits. There may also be tax consequences to consider.
- A reverse mortgage makes it difficult to pass your home on to your heirs after your death; instead the home usually will go to the lender when you move or if you die.

You can receive free information about reverse mortgages by calling AARP at 1-800-209-8085, toll-free. Also see www.aarp.org.

"QUICK MONEY" CHOICES THAT ARE LIKELY TO GET YOU IN DEEPER TROUBLE

In addition to the home equity loans discussed above, we've listed below some other common sources of "quick cash" and what you should know about them. This is just a partial list. More detailed information can be found in NCLC's *Guide to Surviving Debt* and *Stop Predatory Lending* publications. Selected consumer education information about high-rate loans is also included on the companion CD Rom.

1. **Payday loans**: Payday loans go by a variety of names, including "deferred presentment," "cash advances," "deferred deposits," or "check loans," but they all work in the same way. You write a check to the lender or sign an authorization for the lender to take money out of your account electronically. The amount on the check equals the amount borrowed plus a fee that is either a percentage of the full amount of the check or a flat dollar amount. The check (or debit agreement) is then held for up to a month, usually until your next payday or receipt of a government check.

    At the end of the agreed time period, you must either pay back the full amount of the check (more than what the lender gave you), allow the check to be cashed, or pay another fee to extend the loan. The difference between the amount of your check and the amount of cash you get in return is interest or a loan fee that the lender is charging you. **These types of short-term loans are always very expensive.**

    For example:

    > **FIVE DAYS OF WORK FOR FOUR DAYS OF PAY? THE HIGH COST OF BORROWING AGAINST YOUR PAY CHECK**
    >
    > You write a check dated in two weeks for $256
    > You get back today $200
    > Interest and charges $56
    > The interest rate for a loan of two weeks is 730%

Compare this 730% interest rate loan to annual interest rates as low as 10%–15% that banks, credit unions, and finance companies charge. The $56 you spend on this short-term loan means that you will have that much less money in your monthly budget.

Some lenders making this type of loan will encourage you to refinance or renew the loan over and over again. Each time, the lender charges more interest and fees. This just makes a bad situation worse. These loans are marketed not only at check cashing stores and other locations but increasingly over the Internet as well.

2. **Refund Anticipation Loans:** Tax refund anticipation lenders advance you money in exchange for your expected tax refund. The loan is for a very short period of time between when your return is filed with the government and when you would expect to get your tax refund.

   The best advice is to avoid tax refund anticipation loans. Be patient and wait for your full refund if at all possible. If you file electronically with direct deposit, you can usually get your return in about 10 days.

   A great way to save money at tax time is to go to a Volunteer Income Tax Assistance (VITA) site. VITA sites provide free tax preparation to low- and moderate-income taxpayers. VITA sites are sponsored by the IRS and can be found in libraries, community centers, and other locations during tax time. For the nearest VITA site, call the IRS general help line at 1-800-TAX-1040 or go to www.tax-coalition.org.

3. **Pawn Shops and Auto Title Pawns.** Pawnbrokers take property from you in exchange for an amount of money that is always less than what the property is worth. If you cannot repay the loan, the pawn shop keeps the property. Usually pawnbrokers will only lend less than one-half of the value of your property so that they can be sure to get their money back if you don't pay. They also charge very high interest rates.

   If you have valuable property you can live without, consider selling it in a more conventional way for its full value. When you get back on track, you can buy a replacement.

   Another type of "pawn" that exists in some states is called an "auto pawn" where you borrow money at very high interest rates (for example, 240% or 360%) and put up your car title as collateral for the loan. This is also a bad idea. An auto pawn is not as simple and hassle free as the title lenders advertise it to be. You can borrow money elsewhere at lower interest rates without putting your car at risk.

Negotiating With Creditors on Your Own

If you can afford to pay something on your credit card debt, but not the full amount, consider negotiating on your own. It is often easier to negotiate with a creditor before your debt is sent to a collection agency, but you can negotiate with collection agencies as well.

Regardless of the type of deal you try to negotiate, be careful about offering too much. Even a small payment to an unsecured creditor is unwise if this prevents payment of your mortgage or rent. There are other, better ways to stop debt harassment as discussed in Chapter 11.

NEGOTIATING TIPS

You may be surprised that you have some power in negotiating with a creditor or collector. Just knowing your rights in this situation can go a long way. Most important, you have the right not to be harassed or abused by debt collectors. Your rights may be different depending on whether a creditor or collection agency is contacting you. These issues are discussed in Chapter 11.

In general, your ability to get an agreement depends on whether the creditor believes you will honor the agreement. Your chances are likely to be much worse if you have set up a payment plan with this creditor in the past and failed to keep making those payments.

When negotiating with a creditor or collector, avoid over-promising. Be realistic about what you can pay and offer that amount. But at the same time, remember that it will not help you much in the long run if you can only pay a very small amount.

Always be sure to get any negotiated deals in writing and keep a copy. If you're uncomfortable negotiating on your own, you might try to find a social worker, trusted friend or relative to help you.

PAYMENT PLANS

Think first about whether you can offer a lump sum or whether you will have to make monthly payments. A lump sum will often be a better deal, but you may not be able to raise the money. Good (and bad) strategies for raising money are discussed in Chapter 5. You should be very careful about making choices, such as payday loans, that may raise some money for you in the short-term, but will likely cause you more problems not too far down the road.

MAKING A DENT IN WHAT YOU OWE

If you decide to negotiate a payment plan, make sure that the amount you pay each month is enough to make a dent in your debt. An exception to this rule might arise if you are desperate to avoid collection efforts that might harm you, or if you need a low payment plan just for a temporary period.

Not all of your monthly payment will go toward reducing the balance on your credit card debt. For example, let's say you owe $1,000. If you pay $50, your debt will not be reduced to $950. Instead, most of the $50 will go toward paying the interest on the loan. This is why it is almost impossible to get out of credit card debt when you make just the minimum payment.

Here is an example from Bankrate.com:

Suppose you have the following credit card debt:

- Balance: $15,000
- Interest rate: 20%
- Minimum monthly payment: 2-1/2% of the balance
- This month's minimum monthly payment: $375
- Next month's minimum monthly payment $372 (it goes down a little each month)

How long will it take to pay this debt off if you just make the minimum payment each month, and how much interest will you have to pay?

- It will take you almost 42 years to pay off the debt.
- It will cost a whopping $29,500 in interest.

What happens if you tighten your belt so you can pay $500 a month on that same debt? You're debt-free in three and a half years, and only out-of-pocket $6,000 for interest.[7]

Credit card fees also prevent you from getting ahead. While most companies no longer charge annual fees, they now charge several different penalty fees including late fees, "over the limit" fees, balance transfer fees, foreign exchange fees and cash advance fees. Late fees are the most common. According to one survey, nearly 60% of consumers had been charged a late fee in the past year.[8] Creditors make a lot of money on fees: revenue from all fees was about $43 billion in 2003, up from about $39 billion in 2002.[9] To make matters worse, all of the major credit card issuers now raise interest rates when you make a late payment.[10]

7. Dorothy Rosen, Ask the Dollar Diva, bankrate.com (April 16, 2001).
8. Cardweb.com, Late Fee Bug (May 17, 2002).
9. Christine Dugas, Credit Card Fees Become Cash Cow, USA Today (July 13, 2004).
10. Amy C. Fleitas, "20 Sneaky Credit Card Tricks," bankrate.com (Nov. 6, 2002).

ADDITIONAL TERMS TO NEGOTIATE

If you decide to negotiate a payment plan, you can discuss much more than just the monthly amount you will pay. You can also negotiate other terms such as:

- **Re-aging:** Re-aging is a way of turning back the clock and wiping away at least some of your negative credit history. For example, you may be three months late with your credit card payments. If you start paying again, you can ask the creditor to re-age your account. This means that your credit history will show that your account was not late at least for those three months. The missed payments should also be forgiven and any late fees from that time period wiped out. You still owe the money, but you are no longer delinquent. Creditors usually require that you make at least two or three timely payments before they will consider re-aging your account. Your account must be at least nine months old and you cannot re-age more than once over a twelve month period or twice in a five year period.

- **Lowering your interest rate.** One small survey by U.S. PIRG found that consumers had great success in convincing their credit card companies to lower their interest rates when the consumers simply called and asked them to do this.[11] The consumers used this simple script:

Hi. My name is _____. I am a good customer, but I have received several offers in the mail from other credit card companies with lower APRs. I want a lower rate on my card, or I will cancel my card and switch companies.

56% of consumers who called lowered their annual percentage rates (APRs), by an average of more than one-third. It is unclear to what extent this will work for consumers who are already in fairly deep trouble when they call. The key factors affecting success were:

- Length of time with a particular card (longer is better)
- Credit limit on that card (a higher limit is better)
- How maxed out you are on that card (less is better)
- How maxed out you are on your other credit cards (less is better)
- Number of times you missed a payment or paid late on debts other than this credit card (fewer is better)

You might also think about going to a credit counselor for help in setting up a repayment plan. In some cases, a creditor might even refer you to a credit counseling agency.

---

11. Bradley Bakake and the State PIRG Consumer Team, Deflate Your Rate: How to Lower Your Credit Card APR (March 2003).

You should be wary of these referrals because in some cases, the agency may be paying a fee to the creditor to encourage it to refer customers to that agency. This is not always the case and the agency may be perfectly legitimate. However, you should not assume that a creditor's referral ensures quality. Chapter 7 will help you decide whether you should seek help from a credit counselor, and, if so, how to find a reputable agency.

Credit Counseling

Seeking professional debt counseling assistance can be a good idea, but you should be very careful. It is extremely difficult to sort out the good credit counseling agencies from the bad. Many agencies are legitimate, but many are simply rip-offs. Even good agencies won't be able to help you much if you're already too deep in financial trouble.

To make matters even more complicated, there are many other types of companies selling services that they advertise as more effective than credit counseling. This chapter includes information on credit counseling. The next chapter discusses other common types of "debt relief" companies.

WHAT IS CREDIT COUNSELING?

Credit counselors used to be mainly small, community organizations. The quality of their services varied, but few marketed their services beyond the immediate community and few tried to pressure consumers into "buying" their services. This is no longer true.

There are very serious problems with the credit counseling industry. For example, nearly every credit counseling agency in the country has non-profit status. However, many are being investigated by the I.R.S. because of evidence that they operate like for-profit businesses rather than non-profits. This means that when an agency tells you it is "non-profit," you cannot assume that it is above board.

Federal and state enforcement agencies are just starting to catch up with the worst agencies. In the meantime, it is largely up to you to figure out whether credit counseling services are likely to be useful for you and then to find a legitimate agency. This chapter includes information to help you through this process.

A legitimate credit counseling agency offers a range of services, including basic budget counseling, educational courses about finances, *and* debt repayment plans. There are a number of different trade associations that include credit counseling agencies as members, including the National Foundation for Credit Counseling (NFCC) and the Association of Independent Consumer Credit Counseling Agencies (AICCCA). Some, but not all, of the trade associations have best practices standards that their members are supposed to follow. These associations also usually require that their agencies be accredited by a third party. The credible trade associations are working to improve their standards. But there is not much information about how rigorously any association enforces its standards. At least until the dust settles in the credit counseling industry, it is best not to assume that a particular agency, regardless of its affiliation, is a quality agency.

Most credit counseling agencies help with credit card debt only. Some will also help you with other types of unsecured debt, such as medical bills, but most focus on credit card debt. If you are behind on secured debts such as mortgage or car loans, you should seek assistance elsewhere. In some cases, credit counseling agencies will have a separate housing counseling unit. Otherwise, if your main problem is your mortgage debt, you should look for a local nonprofit housing counseling organization. The Department of Housing and Urban Development (HUD) maintains a database of HUD-approved counseling agencies. A list of those agencies can be obtained by calling HUD at (888) 466-3498 or by visiting HUD's web site at www.hud.gov.

HOW CREDIT COUNSELING AGENCIES STAY IN BUSINESS

Most agencies receive a lot of their funding from creditors. This is through a process called Fair Share through which creditors voluntarily return to the agency a set percentage of the funds that are disbursed to them. For example, you might have a debt repayment plan where you pay $100 each month to the credit counseling agency for your Visa bill. If Visa's Fair Share to the agency is 5%, it will credit you with a $100 payment but will actually keep only $95. It will return the extra $5 to the credit counseling agency.

Some agencies will tell you that they receive funding from creditors. Others will not. The important point to remember is that an agency is not necessarily bad just because it receives money from creditors. However, this arrangement does create the possibility of conflicts of interest. Agencies may, for example, be reluctant to advise you to consider bankruptcy even if it is in your best interest because it is not in the interest of your creditors.

Most credit counselors also require consumers to pay fees directly to them. Some may have a sliding scale so that the lowest-income consumers pay less or even nothing at all. Beware of agencies that charge very high monthly and up-front or set-up fees. Some agencies will tell you that they don't charge anything, but will then pressure you to make a "voluntary" contribution. You should avoid these attempts to get you to pay a lot of money for counseling services. Be prepared to ask very specific questions about how much the agency will charge you for different types of services.

Debt Management Plans

Through debt management plans (also called DMPs), you send the credit counseling agency a monthly payment, which the agency then distributes to your creditors. In return, your creditors usually agree to waive fees and reduce interest rates. The creditor will often agree to re-age the account as well. Re-aging is a way of eliminating late fees and negative credit reports that is described in Chapter 6. Another advantage of a debt management plan is that it allows you to make only one payment to the agency rather than having to deal with multiple creditors on your own.

Debt management plans can be helpful for many consumers. For others, they are a terrible idea. The problem is that many agencies will pressure you into a debt management plan whether it makes sense for you or not. A good agency will talk to you about whether a debt management plan is appropriate for you rather than assume that it is.

The challenge for you is to figure out BEFORE you go to a credit counselor whether a debt management plan will be right for you. The more prepared you are ahead of time, the less likely you will get into trouble.

Most creditors offer the same types of terms through debt management plans regardless of which agency they are dealing with. Beware of an agency that tells you it has special connections with a particular creditor and can get you a better deal.

The effect of a debt management plan on your credit report varies significantly depending on your current credit situation. If you are considering credit counseling because you are behind in paying your debts, your credit score and your credit report have probably already been negatively affected. The mere fact that you are participating in a debt management plan will probably not make your *credit score* worse. However, if a potential creditor pulls your *full credit report* rather than just getting your credit score, the report will probably reveal that you are participating in a debt management plan, and that creditor might hold it against you. For more information about credit scores and credit reports, see Chapter Two.

A debt management plan is often pushed as a way of avoiding bankruptcy. This may turn out to be true if a plan is right for you. However, there are two very important points to keep in mind if you think that a debt management plan will keep you out of bankruptcy court:

- Bankruptcy is not necessarily to be avoided at all costs. In many cases, bankruptcy may actually be the best choice for you. This is discussed in Chapter 9.
- If you sign up for a debt management plan that you can't afford, you may end up in bankruptcy anyway.

IS A DEBT MANAGEMENT PLAN
LIKELY TO HELP YOU?

Below are a few questions to ask to help you figure out whether a debt management plan is right for you.

✓ CHECKLIST

1. **Are you having trouble mainly with secured debts? Yes ❑   No ❑**

    If you answered yes, a debt management plan is not likely to help you. There may be an exception to this general rule if you are only slightly behind on your secured debts. In that case, reducing your payments on your unsecured debts might free up extra money to help you pay your secured debts. Just remember that a debt management plan will not directly help you with your secured debt problems.

2. **Do you have little or no money available to pay your credit card debts after you pay your basic living expenses each month? Yes ❑   No ❑**

    If you answered yes, a debt management plan is not right for you.

3. **Are you still current on your credit cards? Yes ❑   No ❑**

    If so, a debt management plan is probably not a good idea. You might be able to improve your situation by taking a budget counseling class and sticking to a tight budget, or by asking your creditors to reduce the interest rate on your cards.

4. **Are you able to pay your priority debts and still have some money left over each month? Yes ❑   No ❑**

    If so, a debt management plan may be helpful. However, be sure to factor in any fees you will have to pay to the agency.

5. **Can you make a long term commitment to making monthly payments? Yes ❑   No ❑**

    If you answered no, a debt management plan will not help you. The drop-out rates for these plans are very high and it is a particularly bad idea to start out thinking that you probably can't complete the plan. Ask the agency to explain to you how long it will take you to pay off your debts through a debt management plan.

6. **Do you want to keep a credit card while on a debt management plan? Yes ❑   No ❑**

    If so, a debt management plan is not for you. Most agencies will require you to stop using any remaining credit cards. Some will allow you to keep one card for emergencies.

The bottom line is that a debt management plan is never a good idea if you do not have any significant amount of money left over each month to pay credit card debt. You still might want to go to a credit counselor just for counseling and educational courses. If you decide to seek help for these reasons, be sure to resist getting lured into a debt management plan. If the agency pressures you to get involved in anything more than counseling and education, you should walk away.

You are only going to benefit from a debt management plan if you have enough money to pay the agency each month. Otherwise, there are alternatives, including bankruptcy that you should consider. Bankruptcy is discussed in Chapter 9.

FINDING A GOOD CREDIT COUNSELING AGENCY

Unfortunately, there are many agencies that do not act in the debtor's best interests. At this point, you cannot assume that a particular affiliation means that an agency offers high-quality services. You cannot assume that any particular promises are true. That doesn't mean stay away. It means go prepared. If you feel at all unsure about the answers you get from a particular agency, move on to another agency.

The ten tips below will help you find an honest agency.

1. **Take the time to shop around.** Making the wrong decision could cost you. You do not need to provide personal financial information in order to find out the basics about an agency. Ask friends and family for referrals. You might also ask a trusted social worker or your local legal services office or other charitable organization. Be careful about claims made in advertising. Many ads are exaggerated and some are even untrue. Call your local Better Business Bureau and the consumer protection office of your state Attorney General's office and rule out agencies that have been the subject of multiple complaints. Some states require agencies to register or get licenses in order to do business in those states. If you live in one of these states, you should check with the state licensing agency about whether the credit counseling agency is licensed and whether there are complaints against the agency.

2. **Consider visiting an agency in-person before signing up.** Although it is sometimes embarrassing or inconvenient to talk face-to-face with counselors, it often leads to a more thorough and direct discussion of your finances than is possible by phone or Internet.

3. **Look for a variety of services.** Seek out an agency that will offer you a range of counseling options, not just enrollment in a debt management plan. The more options the agency offers, the more likely it will be able to offer you assistance that fits your needs. Ask them if they offer budget counseling, savings and debt management

classes, or other educational options. Ask them directly if they will tell you if you should consider options other than a debt management plan, such as bankruptcy or managing your own finances.

4. **Check out all costs.** Most agencies offer similar "deals" from creditors to reduce your debt, but their fees can vary quite a bit. Find out what the agency charges to set up your debt management plan (get a specific dollar amount) and for a monthly fee. Ask them if any of the fees are voluntary, or if they offer lower fees for customers in serious financial hardship. Get a specific quote in writing.

5. **Non-profit status or an affiliation with a particular trade group does not guarantee quality.** Non-profit status does not guarantee affordable fees or quality services. Nearly all credit counseling agencies have non-profit status, including those that take advantage of consumers.

6. **Demand good customer service.** The training and skill of agency employees can mean the difference between effective and shoddy credit counseling. Find out if the employees you are dealing with have taken actual courses in subjects like credit, budgeting and savings, not just a few weeks of training. Make sure the employee spends a good deal of time carefully evaluating all of your debts, not just your credit card bills, and looks at your pay stubs and bills before recommending a counseling plan to you. Find out if the agency provides assistance after you enroll in a debt management plan, such as one-on-one counseling.

7. **Ask about privacy.** Make sure the agency does not sell or distribute any information about your account to others without your permission.

8. **Find out about employee compensation.** Ask employees directly if they are paid more if they sign you up for a debt management plan. Consider going elsewhere if they say yes.

9. **Get the specifics on credit concessions.** Ask the agency if it will deal with all of your unsecured creditors, not just those that pay the agency a fee. Find out exactly how much lower your monthly credit card balance will be and how long it will take to pay off your bills. You should also ask about how credit counseling will affect your credit report or score.

10. **Keep an eye on the agency after you sign up.** If you sign up for a debt management plan, it is best not to stop paying your bills until the plan has been approved by your creditors. Make sure that the agency's payment schedule allows your debts to be paid before they are due each month. Call each of your creditors the first month to make sure they have been paid on time by the agency.

Shopping for a Credit Counseling Agency: A Checklist

Below is a checklist to take with you when you first visit an agency or to use when you contact an agency by phone or Internet.

✓ CHECKLIST

1. Will you keep any information I give you confidential?

   Yes ❏ No ❏

2. What services do you offer? (check all that apply)

   ❏ **Counseling**
   ❏ **Classes on debt management and other issues**
   ❏ **Debt management plans**
   ❏ **Referrals to bankruptcy professionals and other services**
   ❏ **Other**

   (If the agency tells you they only consolidate credit cards or offer debt management plans, don't go there)

3. How much do you charge, if anything, for services?

   Counseling _____
   Education/classes _____
   Debt management plans _____
   Other _____

4. Do your charges include any "voluntary fees"? **Yes ❏ No ❏**

   Do you charge such fees? **Yes ❏ No ❏**

5. Do you have a sliding scale for fees? **Yes ❏ No ❏**

6. Let me tell you a little bit about my situation. What do you think my best options are?

   ❏ **Counseling and budget advice**
   ❏ **Classes/Education**
   ❏ **Debt Management Plan**
   ❏ **Bankruptcy**
   ❏ **Referrals**
   ❏ **Other** _____

   _____

   _____

7. Let me tell you who my creditors are. Do you work with all of these creditors?

   Yes ❑ **No** ❑

   If no, who don't you work with?

   _____

   _____

   What are the typical concessions each of these creditors gives to consumers who sign up for debt management plans?

   Creditor _____ **Typical Concession** _____

   Creditor _____ **Typical Concession** _____

   Creditor _____ **Typical Concession** _____

   Creditor _____ **Typical Concession** _____

8. Can you help me with my secured debt problems?

   Yes ❑ **No** ❑

9. Do you provide training for your counselors? (Please describe)

   Yes ❑ **No** ❑

10. Are your counselors paid by commission?

    Yes ❑ **No** ❑

COMPLAINTS ABOUT CREDIT COUNSELING AGENCIES

The advocate's section at the end of this workbook includes detailed information about possible remedies against credit counseling agencies. At a minimum, if you believe you have been ripped off, you should contact the following:

- Your local consumer affairs office
- State Attorney General's office
- The Federal Trade Commission
- Internal Revenue Service if the agency is a non-profit (and most are).

You may also want to consult a lawyer.

Other Debt Relief Companies

There are a lot of companies trying to make money off of people in debt. These companies know that consumers in debt trouble often feel desperate. They make outrageous claims about supposedly magic solutions to debt problems. These claims are designed to pressure you to buy services that can be very expensive and will often get you even deeper in trouble. The truth is that the road to financial recovery usually takes time and is almost never easy. Keep this in mind as you sort through the claims of debt relief companies.

DEBT SETTLEMENT COMPANIES

Unlike credit counseling agencies, most debt settlement and debt negotiation agencies are for-profit businesses. Negotiation and settlement services are different from debt management services mainly because the debt settlement agencies do not send regular monthly payments to creditors. Instead, these agencies generally maintain your funds in separate accounts, holding your money until the agency believes it can settle your debts for less than the full amount owed.

Here's how a typical debt settlement deal works. You go to the agency because you are behind on credit card debt. In some cases, if you are not yet far enough behind on your debts, they will tell you to stop making payments for a while and then come back.

The companies have different ways of doing business, but nearly all of them will require you to set money aside each month. Sometimes the company will set up an account for you. In other cases, they will ask you to show proof that you have set up your own account. They will almost always figure out a way to take their fees directly from these accounts.

They will require you to deposit a certain amount of money in the account each month. This is intended to build up a fund that can later be used to try to settle your debts. In the meantime, you will not be making any payments on your debts. This means that you could be sued for collection or could be facing pressure from debt collectors to pay. Some debt settlement companies will tell you about your right to be free from debt collection harassment, but most of their employees or "counselors" are not attorneys and cannot help you if you get into trouble that requires legal assistance. More information about responding to debt collectors can be found in Chapter 11.

The companies usually claim that they will stay in contact with your creditors while you are depositing money in your account. They claim that they will monitor the account and will let you know when they think there is enough money to try to make a settlement.

If they are able to work out a settlement with your creditor, they will almost always take a percentage of what you save as a fee. This fee is in addition to the fees that they charge you to start the service and monthly fees they usually take from your account.

Trying to settle your debt may be a strategy that works for you. This option is discussed in Chapter 6. The problem is that the debt settlement business model is rarely the best way to accomplish this. You are likely to end up paying very high fees, among other problems.

A debt settlement agency is also not likely to be of much help if you have a lot of debts. These agencies will generally try to settle your debts, if they do this at all, one at a time. If you have a lot of debts, this could be a very long process. In the meantime, you will not be paying all of your other creditors. This means that those creditors could sue you or keep trying to collect from you in other ways. Also, even if one debt is settled, your credit report will still show that you are in default on your other debts.

If you have just one or maybe two debts and have the money to try to settle those debts, it is best to try negotiating on your own or finding an agency that is willing to help you without charging you high fees and without requiring you to pay them up-front.

Information about legal claims against debt settlement companies can be found in the advocate's section of this workbook and on the CD-Rom.

DEBT TERMINATION OR ELIMINATION COMPANIES

"Debt termination" or "debt elimination" companies claim to be able to eliminate your debt, usually through the use of specially prepared documents. The documents include fake financial papers that claim to eliminate your debt obligations. Some of the documents question the legitimacy of government agencies such as the Federal Reserve Board or even of U.S. currency itself. The documents have different titles, including "Declaration of Voidance," "Bond for Discharge of Debt," and "Redemption Certificate." Some claim to wipe out mortgage debt rather than credit card debt. Another scheme involves sending a series of letters to your creditors to set an arbitration hearing. The companies claim that the creditor will be unable to prove that you owe the money and so your debt can be cancelled.

The Federal Reserve Board and other federal agencies have announced that these schemes are complete frauds. Do not be fooled by their outrageous claims.

CREDIT REPAIR COMPANIES

Credit repair agencies are also called credit clinics or credit service organizations. These companies charge unreasonable fees for services that they claim will help you improve your credit. At best, these businesses are charging you for work you can do yourself for free. More often, they are making promises to improve your credit that they cannot keep. At worst, they will get you involved with rip-off businesses or even, in some cases, in schemes that can later cause you serious legal problems.

Beware of these common erroneous claims made by credit repair companies;

"We can erase bad credit"

The truth is that no one can erase bad credit information from your report if it is accurate.

"Only we can remove old or inaccurate information"

The truth is that if there are legitimate errors on a report or old information, consumers can correct the report themselves for free.

"The bad information on your report is accurate but we'll erase it anyway"

The truth is that if this means lying to the credit reporting agency, it is illegal.

There is a federal Credit Repair Organizations Act (CROA) and many states have laws that can be used to challenge the abusive practices of credit repair agencies. These claims are discussed in the advocates section.

Bankruptcy

9

Bankruptcy can help you eliminate most of your debts and get a fresh start. It can also stop a foreclosure on a home, restore utility service, or undo a wage garnishment.

This chapter is only meant to be an introduction to bankruptcy. If after reading this chapter, you are seriously considering bankruptcy, you should speak with an attorney familiar with bankruptcy or a paralegal working for an attorney.

You should decide to file for bankruptcy only after determining that bankruptcy is the best way to deal with your financial problems. Each case is different. This determination will require careful analysis and depend on a number of factors, many of which are discussed below.

YOUR FEELINGS ABOUT BANKRUPTCY

You may have feelings that make you hesitant to file bankruptcy. Certainly the majority of credit counselors or other companies you go to for help will most likely advise you to avoid bankruptcy at all costs. You should try to balance any negative feelings about bankruptcy with other considerations, such as the need to provide your children with food, clothing and shelter. You should also know that the U.S. Constitution includes a provision for bankruptcy, and that many big corporations and famous people have chosen to file for bankruptcy. In addition, the Bible mentions the need for debt-forgiveness, which sounds a lot like bankruptcy.

If you decide that you do not want to file bankruptcy or the consequences of not paying your credit card debts seem too high for you, we suggest that you go back to the earlier sections of this workbook and see if you can tighten your budget and possibly negotiate with creditors or seek a reputable credit counseling agency to help you pay back your debt.

WHAT IS BANKRUPTCY?

Bankruptcy is a legal proceeding in which a person who cannot pay his or her bills can get a fresh financial start. The right to file for bankruptcy is provided by federal law, and all bankruptcy cases are handled in federal court. Filing bankruptcy immediately stops all of your creditors from seeking to collect debts, at least until your debts are sorted out according to the law.

What Can Bankruptcy Do for You?

Bankruptcy may make it possible for you to:

- Eliminate the legal obligation to pay most or all of your debts. This is called a "discharge" of debts. It is designed to give debtors a fresh financial start.

- Stop foreclosure on a house or mobile home for enough time so that you can catch up on missed payments. (However, bankruptcy does not usually eliminate the mortgage and other liens.)

- Prevent (at least temporarily) repossession of a car or other property, or force the creditor to return property even after it has been repossessed.

- Stop wage garnishment, debt collection harassment, and similar creditor actions to collect debts.

- Restore or prevent termination of utility service.

- Allow you to challenge the claims of creditors who have committed fraud or who are otherwise trying to collect more than you really owe.

- Prevent government agencies from recovering public assistance or Social Security overpayments, unless the receipt of the overpayment was deliberate.

What Bankruptcy Cannot Do

Bankruptcy cannot cure every financial problem. Nor is it the right step for every individual. In bankruptcy, it is usually **not** possible to:

- Eliminate certain rights of "secured" creditors such as those who have a mortgage on your house or a security interest in your car. You can force secured creditors to take payments over time in the bankruptcy process and bankruptcy can eliminate the obligation to pay any additional money if the property is taken. Nevertheless, you generally cannot keep the collateral unless you continue to pay the debt.

- Discharge types of debts singled out by the bankruptcy law for special treatment. These include child support, alimony, certain other debts related to divorce, debts incurred by fraud, most student loans, court restitution orders, criminal fines, and some taxes.

- Protect cosigners on a debt. When a relative or friend has co-signed a loan, and you discharge the loan in bankruptcy, the cosigner may still have to repay all or part of the loan.

- Discharge debts that arise after bankruptcy has been filed.

Although credit card debt can usually be eliminated in bankruptcy, this may not be true if you run up big bills or take cash advances just before filing. Creditors have also sometimes persuaded courts that if you used a credit card at a time when you did not have the intent to repay, you have committed a fraud which prevents the debt from being eliminated in the bankruptcy process.

DIFFERENT TYPES OF BANKRUPTCY

There are two types of bankruptcy cases that are most appropriate for consumer debtors:

Chapter 7

Chapter 7 is known as "straight" bankruptcy or "liquidation." It requires you to give up property which exceeds certain limits called "exemptions," so the property can be sold to pay creditors.

In a bankruptcy case under Chapter 7, you file a petition asking the court to discharge your debts. The basic idea in a Chapter 7 bankruptcy is to wipe out (discharge) your debts in exchange for giving up your property, except for exempt property which the law allows you to keep. In most cases, much or all of your property may be exempt. Property which is not exempt is sold and the money distributed to creditors.

Chapter 13

Chapter 13 is called "debt adjustment". It requires you to file a plan to pay debts (or parts of debts) from current income.

In a Chapter 13 case, you file a plan showing how you will pay off some of your past-due and current debts over an extended period, normally three years. This is different from a Chapter 7 bankruptcy, where you ask the court to wipe out (discharge) your debts.

The most important thing about a Chapter 13 case is that it can allow you to keep valuable property- especially your home-which might otherwise be lost. You should consider filing a Chapter 13 plan if you:

- own your home and are in danger of losing it because of money problems;

- are behind in debt payments, but can catch up on the most important debts if given some time; and

- have regular income. (This can include government benefits such as Social Security). You will need to have enough income in Chapter 13 to pay for necessities and to keep up with the required payments as they come due.

THE TIMING OF YOUR BANKRUPTCY FILING

You may have no choice other than to file immediately to prevent a foreclosure, repossession, eviction, execution sale, or utility shut-off. In an emergency, a bankruptcy case can be filed with as little as ten minutes' preparation. A good discussion of how to do this is set out in the National Consumer Law Center's *Consumer Bankruptcy Law and Practice.* We recommend doing this on your own only in emergencies. It is best to get legal assistance. Resources to help you find legal assistance are included in the bibliography.

As a general rule, you should not file bankruptcy until your debts have peaked. If you do not have medical or automobile insurance, you should try to obtain insurance coverage before filing bankruptcy. If you are unemployed, it is best to file bankruptcy after you have found a new job, in case your lack of income causes you to fall behind on utility bills, rent, or other obligations.

If you decide to wait to file bankruptcy, you must avoid the temptation to obtain goods or services on credit which you do not intend to pay for. In a Chapter 7 bankruptcy, debts incurred in this way can be declared nondischargeable. Debts for prebankruptcy vacation trips and credit card shopping sprees have frequently been found to be nondischargeable. Expenses for medical bills and other essentials are rarely challenged.

Timing is particularly important with Chapter 7 cases as you are not allowed to file again if you received a discharge in a case begun within the past six years.

EFFECT ON YOUR CREDIT REPORT

There is no clear answer as to how a bankruptcy will affect your credit. However, if you are behind on your bills, your credit rating is probably already quite bad. Bankruptcy will probably not make things any worse. The fact that you have filed a bankruptcy can appear on your credit record for ten years. In contrast, defaults may appear for up to seven years. However, since bankruptcy wipes out your old debts, you are likely to be in a better position to pay your current bills and you may be able to get new credit because you no longer have a number of debts in default.

In some cases, a bankruptcy on your record may cause other problems. For example, if you want to work at a bank or certain other jobs, your employer will usually look at your credit report and may ask you about your bankruptcy. But even without a bankruptcy on your record, a poor credit report still might be counted against you. In addition, there are laws that protect you from post-bankruptcy discrimination by the government and at least some types of discrimination by private employers. For more information, see National Consumer Law Center's manual, *Consumer Bankruptcy Law and Practice*.

Congress is very likely to pass drastic changes to bankruptcy law that will likely take effect in late 2005. The new law will make it more difficult for many consumers to discharge debts in bankruptcy. You should consult an attorney for more information. Additional resources are listed in the bibliography at the back of this book.

SECTION THREE:

Possible Consequences of Not Paying

 CHAPTER 10: Understanding the Consequences of Not Paying Your Credit Cards

 CHAPTER 11: Dealing with Debt Collection Harassment

Understanding the Consequences of Not Paying Your Credit Cards

You may decide that you can't afford to make your credit card payments. Before moving forward, you should first try to deal with any feelings of embarrassment or humiliation you may have. As we stated at the beginning of this workbook, you are not alone if you are in trouble with your credit card debts. Economic times are hard and many people find themselves in the same boat as you are.

Feeling a responsibility to pay back your debts is generally a good thing. However, there are times when this is not possible or reasonable. You may be in trouble because of no fault of your own, such as an unexpected illness or job lay-off. There are laws to protect you in these situations and you should not feel embarrassed about using these protections. However, you should also be aware of the consequences of these decisions. These are discussed in this section.

There are three main actions that a creditor or collector can take to try to force you to pay.

1. **Stop Doing Business With You.** For example, a credit card issuer can cancel your card or a dentist to whom you owe money might refuse to let you continue as a patient. Usually, though, there are other merchants or professionals who will offer the same goods or services on a cash basis or even on credit. The threat of stopping business with you is greatest where a particular creditor has a monopoly in your community, such as the only doctor in a rural area. There are also issues to consider if you are behind on your utility bills. More information about utility issues can be found in NCLC's publications *Guide to Surviving Debt* and *Access to Utility Service*.

2. **Report the Default to a Credit Reporting Agency.** The fact that you are behind on your bills almost certainly will end up on your credit record. You cannot stop this, short of always being current on all of your bills. While this is unfortunate, you only make matters worse by paying a particular bill first just because that collector is threatening to ruin your credit record.

The reason you make matters worse is that the collection agency threatening to ruin your credit is almost always bluffing. If a creditor routinely reports delinquent debts to a credit bureau, the damage has most likely already been done. If the creditor does not normally report information to a credit bureau, it is not likely to start with you.

Many creditors never threaten to ruin your credit record. However, they automatically report to a credit bureau by computer every payment and delinquency on a monthly basis. So if you pay a creditor that threatens you rather than one that does not, you may end up with a problem on your credit record anyway.

3. **Begin a Lawsuit to Collect the Debt.** This is the threat that may worry you the most, but the threat of a lawsuit may be much less serious than you imagine.

First, it is hard to predict whether a particular creditor will actually sue on a past-due debt. How aggressively a collection agency threatens suit is no indication whether the creditor will actually sue, even if the threat appears to come from an attorney.

Second, if the creditor does decide to sue you, you have a right to respond and raise any legitimate defenses. Do not let the creditor win by default. You do not have to hire an attorney to respond to the lawsuit, although you should try to do so if possible. Often when a creditor sees that you will contest the action, it will stop pursuing the lawsuit.

Third, even if the creditor does pursue the lawsuit and eventually wins, the worst that can happen is that a court judgment will be entered against you. You will **not** automatically be in contempt of court for failure to pay the judgment. The judgment only gives the creditor the legal right to start the process of **trying** to take back your property, to garnish your wages, or to seek a court order requiring payment.

If you are "judgment proof," you have nothing to fear from even these special collection techniques. You are "judgment proof" if all your assets and income are protected by law from a creditor trying to enforce a court judgment. For example, in most states creditors are not allowed to take your home unless it is worth more than a certain amount. The amount varies greatly from state to state. Other types of property are also exempt, such as a portion of your wages and money in your bank accounts.

Being "judgment proof" is not a permanent condition. If your financial situation improves, the creditor may still be able to collect money from you in the future.

You should figure out whether you are judgment proof as soon as a lawsuit is filed, or—better yet—as soon as a lawsuit is threatened. If you can be hurt by a judgment, there is even more incentive to defend against the lawsuit. To understand whether you can be hurt, you will need to know about state and federal exemption laws. These laws can be very complicated. You should get professional legal advice to help you. At a minimum, you should try to find a publication that explains your state exemption laws.

Even if you are judgment proof, in some extreme cases, you may face further problems. While you cannot be put in jail for failing to pay ordinary debts, a collection tactic usually called a body attachment (also known as a civil arrest warrant, bench warrant or writ of capias) can actually lead to your arrest. Collectors rarely use this extreme tactic, but it can happen if you fail to appear in court when you are ordered to do so. This is a major reason why you should always respond to court papers that you receive and meet all deadlines to file responses or to appear in court.

If you are not judgment proof, you should understand that you may be vulnerable if a creditor decides to sue you. It is best to seek legal advice to help you figure out whether the ways in which a creditor can hurt you are worse than the costs of trying to keep paying your credit card debt. This is also a good time to seriously think about whether bankruptcy is a good choice for you.

Dealing with Debt Collection Harassment

HOW TO AVOID HARASSMENT?

Federal law and many states prohibit harassment by collection agencies (and in some states by creditors). In many cases, the state laws provide additional protections. For example, the federal law applies only to third-party collectors. Some state laws, in contrast, also cover creditors collecting their own debts.

If you are being harassed by debt collectors, you should consider the following eight steps. In most cases, you will want to consider more than one.

1. **Try to Head off Harassment Before it Starts**

    While you should pay your most important bills first, you should not totally ignore any of your bills. Instead, there are steps you can take short of payment which will make it clear to the creditor that you are not ignoring the bill.

    It is to your advantage to try to deal with the problem before the creditor refers the debt to a collection agency. You should consider calling up the creditor to explain your situation. Promptly contacting the creditor is most important with hospitals, doctors, dentists and similar creditors who would otherwise quickly turn a debt over to a collection agency.

    If a certain bill is less important, explain to a creditor why you are not paying and when you propose to pay. You should try to make it clear that you cannot afford to pay the bill and will not pay a collection agency either. Do not over-promise, but be polite and honest. Make sure the creditor understands you will pay as soon as you can so that there is no need to go to the expense of hiring a collection agency.

    The creditor then has a financial interest **not** to turn the matter over to a collector. Collection agencies usually charge the creditor a fee of approximately one-third of what they collect or sometimes charge the creditor a flat fee per debtor. The creditor can avoid this fee by sitting tight.

    You may also have decided that you would like to try to work out a payment plan with the creditor. There are many ways to do this—you may want to negotiate with a creditor on your own, consider paying the creditor back through a debt management plan arranged by a credit counseling agency or try to settle the debt by offering a lump sum. You can find some tips for negotiating on your own in Chapter 6. Credit counseling is discussed in Chapter 7.

2. **The Cease Letter.** Assuming you called the creditor or collector and didn't get anywhere, the simplest strategy to stop collection harassment is to write the collector a cease letter. Your rights will vary depending on whether you are dealing with your creditor or with a collection agency.

Federal law requires collection agencies to stop their collection efforts (sometimes referred to as **dunning**) after they receive a written request to stop. The federal law does not apply to creditors collecting their own debts, but even these creditors will often honor such requests.

You do not have to give any special explanation why the collector should stop contacts. Nevertheless, it is generally a good idea to explain why you cannot pay and your hopes for the future. The letter might also describe any abusive tactics of the collector's employees and any distress this has caused you. It is very important to keep a copy of the written request and to send it by certified mail (return receipt requested). This will give you proof that the collector received your letter.

Here is an example of such a letter:

SAMPLE "CEASE" LETTER

```
                                        Sam Consumer
                                        10 Cherry Lane
                                        Flint, MI 10886

                                        January 1, 2005

NBC Collection Agency
1 Main Street
Flint, MI 10887

Dear Sir or Madam:

I am writing to request that you stop contacting me about an
account number _____ with [name of creditor] as required
by the Fair Debt Collection Practices Act 15 U.S.C. section
1692c(c). [Note: Delete reference to the Act where the let-
ter is to a creditor instead of to a collection agency. Some,
but not all, state laws prohibit further contact by credi-
tors.]
    [Document any harassing contact by the collection agency.
In some cases, provide information about why you can't pay
the bill, or if appropriate, do not owe the money].
    This letter is not meant in any way to be an acknowledg-
ment that I owe this money. I will take care of this matter
when I can. Your cooperation will be appreciated.

Very truly yours,

Sam Consumer
```

Even though it is against the federal law, not all debt collectors will stop contacting you after they receive your letter. You should try not to let them get away with this. If necessary, send another letter and once again keep a copy. Let them know that you are aware that they are violating the federal law by continuing to contact you. You should also keep a careful record of any letters and phone calls you receive after sending the letter. This record may help you if you later decide to sue the debt collector.

You should also consider other options if the debt collector ignores your letter. In particular, you might think about contacting a lawyer to send a letter on your behalf (#3 below), complaining to a government agency about the collector's conduct (#6 below), or suing the debt collector (#8 below).

3. **The Lawyer's Letter.** You do not need a lawyer to send a cease letter. When your main goal is to get the bill collectors off your back, you can send a simple cease letter without the cost of legal assistance. However, if a cease letter does not stop collection calls, a letter from a lawyer usually will. In addition, the lawyer may be able to raise legal claims on your behalf for violations of the federal law that prohibits debt collection harassment.

   Federal law requires collection agencies to stop contacting a consumer known to be represented by a lawyer, as long as the lawyer responds to the collection agency's inquiries. Even though this requirement does not apply to creditors collecting their own debts, these creditors also will usually honor requests from a lawyer. A lawyer working for a creditor or collection agency also is generally bound by legal ethics not to contact debtors represented by a lawyer.

4. **Negotiate with the Creditor or Collector as Discussed in Chapter 6.**

5. **Raise Complaints About Billing Errors and Other Defenses.** Collection letters often contain errors, sometimes misstating the amount due or the account number, or billing the consumer instead of his or her insurance company. Occasionally, you may even receive collection letters aimed at someone with the same or a similar name. When a collection letter contains a mistake, write to request a correction. Collection agencies, by law, must inform you of your right to dispute the debt. They must do this the first time they communicate with you or within five days after first communicating with you about the debt. If you then dispute the debt in writing within the next thirty days, the collection agency must stop collection efforts while it investigates.

   If the dispute involves a line of credit, a credit card, or an electronic transfer of money, you have the additional legal right under the federal Fair Credit Billing Act **to require** the creditor **to investigate** the bill. These issues are discussed in Chapter 4. Additional information is available on the CD-Rom.

There are many other defenses to repayment you should also consider. These include:

- That money was paid by you but not credited to the account;
- That the debt is not owed or that you are current on your payments;
- That the creditor miscalculated the amount due. For example, the creditor may be seeking attorney's fees or collection costs that are too high or possibly not allowed by law;
- That the debt was incurred so long ago that under state law the creditor has waited too long to bring the lawsuit.

You do not need to wait until you are sued to raise possible claims and defenses. In fact, it is usually best to raise all available complaints as early as possible in the debt collection process. Waiting too long may make you less believable later. You should mention your claims every time a creditor or collector contacts you about payment. If the creditor still pursues a lawsuit, raise the claims at that point as well.

If you believe you have claims against a creditor, it is a good idea to put those claims in writing and mail them to the creditor, collector, and any attorneys representing them. This is especially important if you believe that you have warranty or similar claims. Don't forget to keep a copy of anything you mail and send by certified mail, return receipt requested.

Collectors will often tell you to go talk to the original seller or to a prior creditor about any problems. Although the collector might not want to hear your complaints, you should tell the collector anyway. It is always better to defend the creditor or collector's attempt to collect a debt than to give the collector the money and then try to get it back from the original seller.

6. **Complaining to a Government Agency.** Another strategy is to write to government agencies responsible for enforcing laws that prohibit debt collection abuse, like the Federal Trade Commission or your state's attorney general's office.

Your letter of complaint should be sent to the Federal Trade Commission's Consumer Response Center at Federal Trade Commission, CRC-240, Washington, D.C. 20580. You can also call the Commission toll-free at 1-877-FTC-HELP (382-4357) or file a complaint on-line at www.ftc.gov. Copies of the letter should also be sent to the consumer protection division within your state attorney general's office, usually in the state capitol, and also to any local office of consumer protection listed in the local telephone book or on the Internet. Addresses can be obtained from a local better business bureau or office of consumer affairs. An example of such a letter follows:

SAMPLE COMPLAINT LETTER

                                              Sam Consumer
                                              10 Cherry Lane
                                              Flint, MI 10886

                                              January 25, 2005

Federal Trade Commission
Bureau of Consumer Protection
Washington, DC 20580

Dear Sir or Madam:

I am writing to complain of abusive debt collection tactics
used by ABC Collection Agency, 1 Main Street, Flint, MI
10887. I request that you investigate this company.

   I was laid off by U.S. Steel two months ago and have not
been able to maintain all payments on all my bills. ABC began
contacting me in December about my account with Amy's
Department Store in Flint. ABC's abusive collection tactics
have included:

1. Telephoning my sister asking her to lend me the balance
   when she does not have anything to do with this account.
2. Calling me at 6:30 a.m. at home.
3. Using offensive language, calling me a "lousy deadbeat."
4. Writing that they would sue me if they did not receive
   payment in ten days. This was a month and a half ago, but
   all they have done since then is to call and to write.
   (A copy of that letter is enclosed.)
5. Continuing to contact me after I sent them a letter asking them to stop. (Enclosed is my letter to them and a
   later letter from them).
6. Billing me for $245 when no more than $185 is owed on the
   account.

My family and I are doing our best to get back on our feet,
and this abuse is very stressful. Your assistance will be
appreciated.

Very truly yours,

Sam Consumer

cc: Attorney General's Office
       Bureau of Consumer Protection
       Lansing, MI

       Flint Office of Consumer Affairs
       Flint, MI

       ABC Collection Agency
       1 Main Street
       Flint, MI 10887

7. **Bankruptcy.** Filing your initial papers for personal bankruptcy instantly triggers the "automatic stay." This is a very powerful tool because it stops all collection activity against you, from collectors, creditors, or even government officials. No further collection activity can proceed unless a particular collector obtains permission from the bankruptcy court. The bankruptcy court will not grant this permission to collectors seeking to contact you about unsecured debts. For this reason, filing for bankruptcy can be a very effective means of stopping debt harassment.

Nevertheless, as a general rule, a bankruptcy filing is not your best strategy where your only concern is debt harassment. Bankruptcy should be saved for when you have serious financial problems. Debt collection harassment can usually be stopped without having to resort to bankruptcy. In fact, be wary of any attorney offering to file bankruptcy for you where the only problem is debt harassment. More detailed information on bankruptcy can be found in Chapter 9.

8. **Sue the Debt Collector for Illegal Conduct.** Federal and state fair debt laws provide you with strong protections from debt collection harassment. Debt collectors often break these rules because they know that in most cases they can get away with it. Most consumers either don't know about their rights or don't have the resources to fight back.

The federal Fair Debt Collection Practices Act (FDCPA) prohibits collectors from engaging in a wide range of abusive and harassing conduct, including:

- Communicating with third parties, such as relatives or friends about a debt unless the court has given the collector permission to do so. There are a few narrow exceptions to this rule.
- Contacting you at work if the collector should know that your employer prohibits personal calls or contacting you at other inconvenient places.
- Falsely representing the character, amount or legal status of a debt.
- Threatening to take actions that are illegal or not intended.
- Failing to disclose in communications that the collector is attempting to collect a debt.

This is only a partial list of FDCPA requirements. More detailed information can be found in NCLC's publication *Guide to Surviving Debt* and *Fair Debt Collection* manual.

SECTION FOUR:

The Road to Financial Recovery

 CHAPTER 12: Checklists to Help You Get Back On Your Feet

Checklists To Help You Get Back On Your Feet

Once you start resolving your financial problems, it is important to make choices for the future which will help you avoid getting into trouble again. These checklists are intended to be used as guides for thinking about your financial life once your current debt problems are resolved.

YOUR BUDGET

You should not give up on your new budget once you are no longer facing a crisis. However, if your financial situation has changed, you should take another look at your budget to see if there is room to make some changes.

When faced with a financial crisis, you learned what your family can do without. In reexamining your budget, keep in mind what your family's true needs are. Here are some suggestions about issues to consider:

- Can you start rebuilding your savings account? **Yes ❑ No ❑**

  Savings is an important part of getting back on your feet. Your savings account can help to protect you against new financial problems if they arise. You might also look into a savings program such as a local America Saves office. For more information about America Saves, see www.americasaves.org or call Consumer Federation of America at (202) 387-6121.

- Did you postpone paying for home maintenance or other necessities?

  Yes ❑ No ❑   These may now be priorities.

- Did you cut back in areas, like auto maintenance, that require special attention in order to prevent future problems? **Yes ❑ No ❑**

- Have you forgotten about any low-priority debts which you now wish to address? **Yes ❑ No ❑**

- Did you reduce or eliminate contributions to a retirement plan or borrow against that plan? **Yes ❑ No ❑**

  Do you need to resume contributions or repay a retirement plan loan in order to provide for a stable retirement? **Yes ❑ No ❑**

- Did you reduce insurance or medical coverage to save money temporarily? Is it necessary to restore the original coverage? **Yes ❑ No ❑**

YOUR CREDIT CARD CHOICES

You are likely to continue to get offers for credit cards despite your recent financial problems. While access to some credit can be necessary, you want to avoid getting back in over your head.

- Have you reduced your reliance on credit card spending? **Yes** ❑ **No** ❑

   Can you start to pay your balance in full each month to avoid new problems?
   Yes ❑ **No** ❑

- Do you have the cheapest available credit card? **Yes** ❑ **No** ❑

   Do you understand all of its terms? Have you called the credit card company and asked for an interest rate reduction? **Yes** ❑ **No** ❑

   (More information about shopping for credit cards can be found on the companion CD-Rom).

- Can you pay more than the minimum amount due so that you keep your balance manageable? **Yes** ❑ **No** ❑

- Have you resolved any disputes about how much is due? **Yes** ❑ **No** ❑

- Are you avoiding easy credit offers that are too good to be true? **Yes** ❑ **No** ❑
   These often contain high fees and hidden penalties.

PROTECTING YOUR HOME OR APARTMENT

CHECKLIST

To make sure that you can keep your home for the long term, here are some things to consider:

- If you have caught up on home mortgage or lease payments, have you reviewed your recent bills to make sure that your mortgage company or landlord agrees that you are caught up? **Yes** ❑ **No** ❑

   Has the lender or landlord properly credited all necessary payments?

   Yes ❑ **No** ❑

   Have all court cases related to foreclosure or eviction been dropped?

   Yes ❑ **No** ❑

- Is your current savings plan sufficient to protect you if urgent home repair needs arise in the future? **Yes** ❑ **No** ❑

   Is your savings plan sufficient to help you get through any new period of financial difficulties? **Yes** ❑ **No** ❑

- If you find that you are continuing to struggle financially, have you thought about moving to a cheaper residence? **Yes** ❑ **No** ❑

Would it relieve pressure for your family if you spent less on housing?
Yes ❑ **No** ❑

∎ Have you implemented utility conservation measures which will make your home less expensive to maintain in the long term? **Yes** ❑ **No** ❑

∎ Have you shopped around for home insurance at the best possible rate?

Yes ❑ **No** ❑

∎ Have you applied for any real estate tax abatement you may be entitled to?

Yes ❑ **No** ❑

∎ Have you received a larger than expected escrow payment increase from your mortgage company? **Yes** ❑ **No** ❑

If you are caught up on back payments, this may be in error. Some mortgage companies are careless about escrow accounting. If you can't get the issue resolved quickly, you may want to see a lawyer.

REBUILDING CREDIT

If you have had financial problems, there are likely to be some things on your credit report which won't go away easily. However, there are some things you can do which may make things easier for you in the future.

❑ Have you checked your credit report to make sure it is accurate? (For more information on how to order a report, see Chapter 2.)

❑ Have you resolved any disputes about your credit report or sent the reporting agencies an explanatory statement to include when they distribute your report?

❑ Are you establishing better credit habits which will show new creditors that you are responsible? Have you tried buying something on time and paying the debt promptly to show potential lenders that you can manage your debts?

❑ Have you canceled unnecessary credit cards and lines of credit which may make new creditors concerned about your potential to become overextended?

❑ Are you still getting credit card solicitations in the mail? Have you limited your-self to one unsecured credit card on the best terms offered?

❑ Have you opted out of pre-screening credit card offers? To do this, call 1-888-5-OPTOUT (1-888-567-8688). In addition, you can notify the three major credit bureaus that you do not want personal information about you shared for promotional purposes. To ask the three major credit bureaus not to share your personal information, write to:

Equifax, Inc.
Options
PO Box 740123
Atlanta, GA 30374-0123

Experian
Consumer Opt-Out
701 Experian Parkway
Allen, TX 75013

TransUnion
Marketing List Opt Out
PO Box 97328
Jackson, MS 39288-7328

❑ Are you shopping around for credit on fair terms? If not, you may be making a mistake. Don't assume that, because one creditor tells you that you are a poor credit risk, others will tell you that as well.

❑ When you apply for credit for big, expensive items, like a home or car, are you providing a good explanation for your financial problems together with evidence showing that they have been resolved?

❑ Are you shopping around for the best deal? It's a good idea to get a quote from a bank or credit union before negotiating with a car dealer or other merchant. For a mortgage loan, shopping around is even more important. You might be able to join a local credit union as well.

❑ Are you worrying about your credit record unnecessarily? Having resolved your financial problems, can you make a decision to reduce your reliance on credit for several years so that you don't have the pressure of new difficulties?

You should also realize that consumer scams are often targeted against people that have had recent financial problems. A company may get your name from bankruptcy court records, foreclosure records, or by purchasing lists from debt collectors. Some of these companies assume that you will be desperate enough to make bad decisions about credit. Be careful.

Most important, before you try to rebuild your credit by getting new credit, make sure that your past financial problems are fully fixed. Don't be too eager to take on new debt. **The most critical step in rebuilding is not necessarily the number of new credit cards that you have but, rather, evidence of your ongoing ability to repay loans or credit.** Perhaps the worst thing you can do for your credit record is to take on too much new credit too soon and fail a second time. It is best to rebuild your credit history by focusing on stabilizing your income and keeping your debt burden low.

Glossary

All terms in italics are defined in this glossary.

Annual Percentage Rate. The interest rate on a loan expressed under rules required by federal law. It is more accurate to look at the annual percentage rate (as opposed to the stated interest rate) to determine the true cost of a loan, because it tells you the full cost of the loan including many of the lender's fees. You will find the annual percentage rate for a loan on the disclosure statement that is given to you when the loan papers are signed.

Attachment. A legal process that allows a creditor to "attach" a *lien* to property that you own. Depending on state law, almost any kind of property may be subject to attachment, including your home, automobile, bank accounts, and wages. Once a *lien* is attached to the property, you may face further collection action on that property, including execution, *garnishment* or *foreclosure.*

Automatic Stay. A bankruptcy case automatically prevents continuation of creditor collection activity. Filing bankruptcy is the only way to get this protection.

Bankruptcy. A legal process available in all states that allows you to address your debt problems according to a set of special rules while getting protection from continued collection activity.

Collateral. Property put up to secure a loan. If you have given a creditor collateral, that creditor can normally take and sell the collateral if you are not able to repay the loan. A creditor with collateral is normally known as a *"secured creditor."*

Cosigner. A person who agrees to be responsible for someone else's debt. A cosigner is normally responsible for paying back a debt just as if he or she had received the money.

Credit Bureau, also called consumer reporting agency or credit reporting agency. This is a company that receives information about a consumer's credit history and keeps records that are available to those seeking data about that consumer.

Credit Report, also called a consumer report or a credit record, is the information about a consumer that a credit bureau has on file that it can report to others.

Credit Score. A credit score is a number that summarizes your credit history. The purpose of the score is to help lenders evaluate whether you are a risky borrower.

Creditor. Any person or business to which you owe money.

Debt Collector. The most common use of this term applies to anyone who collects debts. However, under the federal Fair Debt Collection Practices Act ("FDCPA"), the term "debt collector" only applies to collection agencies and lawyers (or their employees) that are collecting debts for others. State laws may cover other types of collectors.

Debtor. Any person who owes money to another. In *bankruptcy,* the term "debtor" refers to the person who begins a bankruptcy case.

Default. Failing to meet the requirements of an agreement. Most defaults involve failure to make required payments.

Defense. A legal reason why a court should not award any or all of what is requested in a lawsuit. For example, a statement that the money is not owed is a defense to a collection lawsuit.

Discharge. A document that ends a debtor's legally enforceable obligation to pay a debt. It is common to get a discharge of a mortgage debt after the mortgage is fully paid off. In addition, most bankruptcies result in a discharge at the end of the case that applies to many debts.

Equity. Your equity in property is the amount of cash you would keep if you sold property and paid off all of the liens on that property. For example, if you own a house worth $100,000, but you owe $60,000 on your original mortgage and $10,000 on a second mortgage, you have $30,000 in equity. The same principle applies to cars and other types of property.

Exempt Property. Property that the law allows you to keep when you are being faced with collection on an *unsecured debt*.

Exemptions. These are laws that give you the right to maintain your *exempt property*.

Federal Law. A law of the United states that applies throughout the country. The *bankruptcy* law is an example of a federal law.

Foreclosure. A legal process to terminate your ownership of real estate that is *collateral* for a debt, based on a *mortgage* or deed of trust. In some states, foreclosure involves a court proceeding ("judicial foreclosure"), while in others foreclosure occurs by creditor action alone ("non-judicial foreclosure").

Garnishment. A creditor's seizure, to satisfy a debt, of property belonging to the *debtor* that is in the possession of a third party. Usually a court has to authorize the seizure in advance. An example would be seizure of money in your bank account to repay a court judgment. Wages owed to you can also be garnished in many states.

Homestead Exemption. The right, available in most states and in the *bankruptcy* process, to treat your residence as *exempt property* that cannot be sold to satisfy the claims of *unsecured creditors*. In most states, the homestead exemption covers a certain dollar amount of your equity in your residence.

Judgment. A determination by a court as to the outcome of a lawsuit, including any amounts owed.

Judgment-Proof. This term is applied to people or businesses with property of minimal value, which can be entirely protected by *exemptions*. If you are judgment-proof, it is difficult or sometimes impossible for any creditor to force you to pay a debt.

Lien. Also called a "security interest," it is a legal interest taken by creditors in your property to secure repayment of a debt. A lien can be created voluntarily in connection with a loan, such as when you pledge real estate by giving a creditor a *mortgage* or deed of trust. A lien can also be created without your consent by *attachment* based on a court order. A creditor with a lien is called a *secured creditor*.

Mortgage. An agreement in which a property owner grants a *creditor* the right to satisfy a debt by selling the property in the event of a *default*.

Negative Amortization. Negative amortization occurs when your payments do not cover the amount of interest due for that payment period.

Note. This term is commonly used as a name for a contract involving the loan of money.

Notice of Right to Cancel. This document explains your right to cancel a loan in some circumstances. You should receive such a notice in connection with most door-to-door sales and for *mortgage* loans that are not used to buy your residence.

Personal Property. Property other than real estate.

Pro Se (also called pro per). Representing yourself (without an attorney) in a legal case or bankruptcy proceeding.

Refinancing. The process of paying back old debts by borrowing new money either from an existing *creditor* or a new creditor.

Repossession (often called "self-help repossession"). Seizure by the creditor of *collateral* after the debtor's *default*, usually without court supervision or permission. Repossession is most common in connection with car loans.

Secured Creditor. Any *creditor* that has *collateral* for a debt.

Secured Debt. A debt for which the *creditor* has *collateral* in the form of a *mortgage, lien,* or *security interest* in certain items of property. The creditor can seize the property *collateral* if the *debtor defaults* in repayment of the debt.

Security Interest. See "*Lien,*" above.

State Law. A law passed by an individual state that only applies to transactions in that state.

Unsecured Creditor. A *creditor* that has no *collateral* for the debt owed.

Unsecured Debt. A debt that does not involve *collateral.*

Wage Garnishment. *Garnishment* of the *debtor's* wages from the debtor's employer.

Bibliography

Recommended NCLC Publications

All National Consumer Law Publications can be ordered from Publications, National Consumer Law Center, 77 Summer Street, Boston, MA 02110, www.consumerlaw.org, (617) 542-9595, Fax (617) 542-8028, publications@nclc.org. See the order form at the back of this volume.

NCLC Books for Consumers

The National Consumer Law Center Guide to Surviving Debt: What a consumer or counselor needs to know about debt collectors, managing credit card debt, debt counseling or debt relief agencies, whether to refinance, credit card problems, home foreclosures, evictions, repossessions, credit reporting, utility terminations, student loans, budgeting, and bankruptcy.

The National Consumer Law Center Guide to Mobile Homes: What consumers need to know about mobile home dealer practices, and what to look for in-depth about mobile home quality and defects, when not to buy a home, what to look for about delivery and installation, how to obtain warranty service, and tips on maintaining a home. Over 30 photographs graphically demonstrate construction details.

The National Consumer Law Center Guide to Consumer Rights for Immigrants: an introduction to many of the most critical consumer issues faced by immigrants, including international wires, check cashing and banking, notario and immigration consultant fraud, affidavits of support, telephones, utilities, credit history discrimination, high-cost credit, used car fraud, student loans and more.

Return to Sender: Getting a Refund or Replacement for Your Lemon Car: Find how lemon laws work, what consumers and their lawyers should know to evaluate each other, how to develop the facts, legal rights, and how to handle both informal dispute resolution proceedings, and more.

National Consumer Law Center Consumer Education Brochures: NCLC has a wide array of brochures, some translated into other languages, that are available at www.consumerlaw.org.

Selected NCLC Books for Lawyers

Consumer Bankruptcy Law and Practice: the definitive personal bankruptcy manual, with step-by-step instructions from initial interview to final discharge, and including consumers' rights as creditors when a merchant or landlord files for bankruptcy. Appendices and CD-Rom contain over 130 annotated pleadings, bankruptcy statutes, rules and fee schedules, an interview questionnaire, a client handout, and software to complete the latest versions of petitions and schedules.

Fair Debt Collection: the basic reference in the field, covering the Fair Debt Collection Practices Act and common law, state statutory and other federal debt collection protections. Appendices and companion CD-Rom contain sample pleadings and discovery, the FTC's Official Staff Commentary, all FTC staff opinion letters, and summaries of reported and unreported cases.

Student Loan Law: student loan debt collection and collection fees; discharges based on closed school, false certification, failure to refund, disability, and bankruptcy; tax intercepts, wage garnishment, and offset of social security benefits; repayment plans, consolidation loans, deferments, and non-payment of loan based on school fraud. CD-Rom and appendices contain numerous forms, pleadings, interpretation letters and regulations.

Fair Credit Reporting: the key resource for handling any type of credit reporting issue, from cleaning up blemished credit records to suing reporting agencies and creditors for inaccurate reports. Covers credit scoring, privacy issues, identity theft, the FCRA, the new FACTA, the Credit Repair Organizations Act, state credit reporting and repair statutes, and common law claims.

Consumer Banking and Payments Law: unique analysis of consumer law (and NACHA rules) as to checks, money orders, credit, debit, and stored value cards, and banker's right of setoff. Also extensive treatment of electronic records and signatures, electronic transfer of food stamps, and direct deposits of federal payments. The CD-Rom and appendices reprint relevant agency interpretations and pleadings.

Credit Discrimination: analysis of the Equal Credit Opportunity Act, Fair Housing Act, Civil Rights Acts, and state credit discrimination statutes, including reprints of all relevant federal interpretations, government enforcement actions, and numerous sample pleadings.

Unfair and Deceptive Acts and Practices: the only practice manual covering all aspects of a deceptive practices case in every state. Special sections on automobile sales, the federal racketeering (RICO) statute, unfair insurance practices, and the FTC Holder Rule.

STOP Predatory Lending: A Guide for Legal Advocates: provides a roadmap and practical legal strategy for litigating predatory lending abuses, from small loans to mortgage loans. The CD-Rom contains a credit math program, pleadings, legislative and administrative materials, and underwriting guidelines.

NCLC REPORTS is a newsletter covers the latest developments and ideas in the practice of consumer law, issued 24 times a year.

Books By Other Publishers

James P. and John M. Caher, *Debt Free* (Owl Books, 1996).
Stephen R. Elias, Albin Renauer, Robin Leonard and Kathleen Michon, *How to File For Chapter Seven Bankruptcy* (Nolo, 11th ed. May 2004).
Evan Hendricks, *Credit Scores and Credit Reports: How the System Works, What You Can Do* (Privacy Times, 2004).
Robin Leonard, *Money Troubles* (Nolo, 9th ed. August 2003).
Robin Leonard, *Credit Repair* (Nolo, 6th ed. August 2002).
Michelle Singletary, *Seven Money Mantras for a Richer Life* (Random House, 2004)
Henry J. Sommer, *Consumer Bankruptcy: The Complete Guide to Chapter 7 and Chapter 13 Personal Bankruptcy* (John Wiley & Sons, 1994).
Howard Strong, *What Every Credit Card User Needs To Know* (Henry Holt & Company, 1999).

Helpful Web Sites

Credit Bureaus

Equifax: www.equifax.com
Experian: www.experian.com
Transunion: www.transunion.com
To order free report: www.annualcreditreport.com

General Consumer and Legal Sites

AARP: www.aarp.org
American Bankruptcy Institute: www.abiworld.org
Better Business Bureau: www.bbb.org
Consumer Action: www.consumer-action.org
Consumer Federation of America: www.consumerfed.org
Consumers Union: www.consumersunion.org
Credit Scoring: www.creditscoring.com (This is a private site that has news and information regarding credit scoring).
National Association of Consumer Advocates: www.naca.net
National Association of Consumer Bankruptcy Attorneys: www.nacba.org
National Consumer Law Center: www.consumerlaw.org or www.nclc.org
Nolo Press: www.nolo.com
Privacy Rights Clearinghouse: www.privacyrights.org
U.S. PIRG: www.uspirg.org

Government Sites

Federal Trade Commission: www.ftc.gov
Government Services Agency: www.pueblo.gsa.gov (The government's consumer information center).
Internal Revenue Service: www.irs.gov
U.S. Department of Education (Information about student financial assistance): www.ed.gov
U.S. Department of Housing and Urban Development: www.hud.gov

Information to Help You Find Legal Assistance

In most communities (or close by if you live in a rural area), there are organizations which provide free legal help to people whose incomes fall below certain amounts.

Many of these programs are funded by the Legal Services Corporation (LSC). You can find out more about programs near you by looking up LSC's web site, www.lsc.gov, or by calling (202) 295-1500. To find out if there are legal services programs in your area that are not funded by LSC, you should check your local phone book or ask a local social services or consumer protection agency. Court clerks often have information about legal services programs as well.

For consumer law problems, you should also look up the National Association of Consumer Advocates (NACA) list of members. NACA's list is divided by region and by area of practice. The members also rate their level of experience in different consumer areas. Contact NACA by calling (202) 452-1989 or check out the NACA web site at www.naca.net. Another helpful resource is the National Association of Consumer Bankruptcy Attorneys, which provides referral lists for local bankruptcy lawyers. You can find out more from their web site, www.nacba.org or by calling (202) 331-8005.

Penn State's Dickinson School of Law maintains a database of pro bono bankruptcy clinics. For more information, see www.dsl.psu.edu.

ADVOCATE'S SECTION

This section includes information about possible legal claims that may apply if a consumer has problems with a debt management, debt settlement, or credit repair agency. Consumer protection laws with respect to credit reports, credit card billings, and fair debt collection are also discussed briefly in this section. More information about these issues, including consumer education brochures, is available on the CD-Rom accompanying this workbook. The CD also contains sample pleadings, extensive detail about state debt management laws, and other important information about the credit counseling industry.

Be advised that the information in this section is likely to change. The best sources for updates are the NCLC manuals cited throughout this workbook.

I. COUNSELING AND REPRESENTING DEBTORS

This section focuses mainly on legal claims that may be brought against unscrupulous debt relief companies. Consumer protection laws that are relevant to debtors are also discussed here. These legal claims should be considered by attorneys representing consumers with credit card debt problems.

There are many other strategies that can be used to assist debtors. In particular, we encourage advocates to go through the information in the consumer section of this workbook with clients. Many consumers will benefit greatly from assistance with filling out the budgeting forms, writing cease letters to collectors, and understanding their exemption rights. Much of this assistance can be provided by non-attorney advocates. It is also important to help clients understand when bankruptcy may be an effective option.

In many cases, counseling services are just as critical as representing consumer debtors in court. Despite the importance of counseling, there is very little information about the elements of effective counseling. Similarly, there are few, if any, effective programs of study for advocates that counsel consumers and debtors. In some cases, advocates may wish to refer clients to local consumer credit counselors or other non-profit counseling agencies. As discussed in detail in this workbook, however, not all non-profit counseling organizations act in the best interests of consumers. Advocates should research possible referrals carefully before recommending them to clients.

Additional Resources

Advocates may also wish to consider taking courses on effective counseling techniques as well as substantive courses on consumer issues. For example, the Coalition for Consumer Bankruptcy Debtor Education in New York City offers "Train the Trainers" programs. For more information, see www.debtoreducation.org. The National Endowment for Financial Education (www.nefe.org) is another resource for consumer education and financial literacy programs. Additional resources to get up to speed on substantive consumer issues are included in the bibliography.

II. LEGAL CLAIMS AGAINST ABUSIVE "DEBT RELIEF" COMPANIES

Introduction

Problems with credit counseling and other debt relief companies are discussed in Chapters 7 and 8 of this workbook. There are a number of possible legal remedies available to challenge these abuses. Key legal claims are discussed in the first half of this section. For more information about credit counseling abuses, see National Consumer Law Center and Consumer Federation of America, Credit Counseling in Crisis, April 2003. The U.S. Senate Permanent Subcommittee on Investigations also released a report in March 2004, Profiteering in a Non-Profit Industry: Abusive Practices in Credit Counseling. Both of these reports are available on the companion CD-Rom. The CD-Rom also contains other useful information about credit counseling and other debt relief companies, including sample pleadings, government enforcement actions, and investigative reports. A detailed, annotated list of state debt management laws is also available on the CD-Rom.

1. Credit Repair Organizations Act

The federal Credit Repair Organizations Act (CROA) applies only to agencies that offer credit repair services.[1] The definition is broad, encompassing any person who performs or offers to perform any service, for a fee or other valuable consideration, for the express or implied purpose of (i) improving any consumer's credit record, credit history, or credit rating or (ii) providing advice and assistance to any consumer with regard to any activity or service described above.[2] Credit repair agencies are clearly covered. Many credit counseling and debt settlement agencies should also fit this definition.

The CROA is a powerful law. It requires agencies to make certain disclosures and also includes numerous substantive protections for consumers. For example, the law specifies terms that must be included in contracts with consumers, including a three day right to cancel.[3]

Violations of the law can lead to extensive consumer remedies. For example, any contract not in compliance with the Act is treated as void.[4] In addition, consumers are entitled to actual damages, punitive damages and reasonable attorney fees.

A critical problem with the CROA and its state analogues is that it does not apply to non-profit organizations.[5] This is particularly a problem in the credit counseling context. Although the vast majority of agencies now charge at least some fees for service, nearly every organization in the industry operates as a non-profit. It may be possible to overcome this hurdle by arguing that a non-profit is a for-profit business in disguise either because it focuses entirely on selling DMPs or because of close connections to for-profit affiliates.[6] Since most debt settlement and credit repair companies are for-profit businesses, the CROA should clearly apply to them.

---

1. 15 U.S.C. § 1679-1679j.
2. 15 U.S.C. § 1679a(3)(A).
3. 15 U.S.C. §1679e.
4. 15 U.S.C. §1679f(c).
5. 15 U.S.C. § 1679a(3)(B)(i).
6. For example, a class action lawsuit against Cambridge Credit Counseling was based primarily on alleged violations of the federal CROA. *See* Zimmerman v. Cambridge Credit Counseling Corp. *et al*, Civ. Action 3:03-cv-30261-MAP, Clearinghouse # 55455 (D. Mass. filed Nov. 4, 2003). However, in 2004, the Massachusetts district court rejected Plaintiffs' arguments that the court should examine whether an agency is truly "non-profit" even if it has been granted that status by the I.R.S. *See* Zimmerman v. Cambridge Credit Counseling Corp., 322 F. Supp. 2d 95 (D. Mass. 2004) (The IRS determination of tax-exempt status was dispositive on the issue of whether providers were exempt from the CROA). *See also* Limpert v. Cambridge Credit Counseling, 328 F. Supp. 2d 360 (E.D.N.Y. 2004) (CROA may apply to credit counseling agencies that make representations regarding credit reports, but claims against 501(c)(3) agencies dismissed due to non-profit exemption).

A thorough discussion of the law can be found in NCLC's publication, Fair Credit Reporting (5th ed. 2002 and Supp.).

2. State Debt Management Laws

Many state laws specifically prohibit the business of debt pooling (also known as debt management plans, debt consolidation, budget planning, or debt prorating). The majority do not specifically provide for private enforcement.[7] Some are contained in the state criminal codes. Where no specific private remedy is provided, violations should be UDAP violations.

With notable exceptions, these state laws are generally ineffective and/or under-enforced.[8] However, a few states stepped up enforcement throughout 2003 and 2004. The state actions generally raised UDAP claims and in some cases claims based on violations of federal and state telemarketing laws or state debt management laws. Selected pleadings from these enforcement actions can be found on the companion CD-Rom.

Some of the state laws explicitly apply to any organization that does business with consumers in that state. Even without this explicit language, advocates should argue that the law should be broadly construed in order to protect consumers in the state.

The state debt management laws vary in scope. About half of the states require some type of licensing for agencies providing debt management services. But nearly half of these states explicitly exempt most non-profits from the licensing requirements. A minority of states restricts debt management business in the state to non-profits and requires these non-profits to be licensed.

The stronger state laws provide regulation beyond licensing and/or regulation. The most common substantive regulations include fee limits and requirements that consumers be given written contracts and that agencies maintain consumer payments in separate trust accounts. In addition, most of the states that require licenses also require agencies to post bonds.

As of 2004, the following states had some type of licensing requirements.[9] More detail about each of these laws can be found on the companion CD-Rom.

1. Arizona: Ariz. Rev. Stat. § 6-701-716.
2. California: Cal. Fin. Code § 12100-12403.
3. Connecticut: Conn. Gen. Stat. § 36a-655-665.
4. Idaho: Idaho Code § 26-2222-2251.
5. Illinois: 205 Ill. Comp. Stat. Ann. § 665/2-665/22.
6. Indiana: Ind. Code § 28-1-29-1-28-1-29-14.
7. Iowa: Iowa Code § 533A.1-533A.15.
8. Kansas: Kan. Stat. Ann. §21-4402. In 2004, Kansas amended its existing debt management law and added a registration requirement, among other substantive provisions. See S.B. #509.

---

7. In an encouraging sign for consumers, a number of states that have recently passed legislation in this area have included an explicit private right of enforcement for consumers. Although these provisions are helpful to consumers, violations of these laws should be UDAP violations regardless of whether this explicit language is included.

8. See National Consumer Law Center, Credit Counseling in Crisis Update: Poor Compliance and Weak Enforcement Undermine Laws Governing Credit Counseling Agencies (November 2004). Available on-line at www.nclc.org/initiatives/credit_counseling/content/cc_enforcement.pdf.

9. Some of the states listed below explicitly exempt non-profits from licensing or registration requirements. Others implicitly exempt at least some non-profit organizations by defining the practice of debt management to include only those organizations that charge fees or receive consideration for services. Thus, the minority of credit counseling agencies that do not charge fees for service are arguably not required to obtain licenses in these states. There is some question whether "voluntary contributions" should be classified as fees or as consideration. Advocates should argue that "voluntary contributions" are rarely voluntary and are the same as fees. For more information about this issue, see the annotated list of state debt management laws on the CD-Rom.

9. Louisiana: Louisiana has two laws governing debt adjusting that contradict each other. One law generally prohibits for-profit debt adjusting, but exempts non-profit organizations. La. Rev. Stat. Ann. § 14:331. A second law allows financial planning and management services, but requires the agencies to be licensed. Non-profits engaging in debt management services are exempted from the licensing requirement. La. Rev. Stat. Ann. § 37:2581-2598.
10. Maine: Me. Rev. Stat. Ann. tit. 17, § 701-703; Me. Rev. Stat. Ann. tit. 32, § 6171-6182.
11. Maryland: Md. Fin. Inst. § 12-901-12-931.
12. Michigan: Mich. Comp. Laws Ann. § 451.411-436.
13. Minnesota: Minn. Stat. § 332.13-332.30.
14. Mississippi: Miss. Code Ann. § 81-22-1-81-22-29
15. Nebraska: Neb. Rev. Stat. § 69-1201-1217.
16. Nevada: Nev. Rev. Stat. § 676.010-676.340.
17. New Hampshire: N.H. Rev. Stat. Ann. § 399-D:1 through D: 28.
18. New Jersey: N.J. Stat. Ann. §§ 2C:21-19, 17:16G-1-16G-8.
19. New York: N.Y. Gen. Business Law. § 455-457; N.Y. Banking Law § 579-587.
20. Ohio: Ohio Rev. Code Ann. § 4710.01-4710.04.
21. Oregon: Or. Rev. Stat. § 697.602-697.990.
22. Rhode Island: R.I. Gen. Law § 19-14-1-19-14.7-4.
23. South Carolina: S.C. Code Ann. § 40-5-370 (Only licensed attorneys may perform debt pooling services for compensation).
24. Vermont: Vt. Stat. Ann. tit. 8, § 4861-4876.
25. Virginia: Va. Code Ann. § 6.1-363.2 through 363.26.
26. Wisconsin: Wis. Stat. § 218.02.

About twenty states take a different, generally less restrictive, approach. Most of these states generally prohibit debt adjusting, but allow a long list of exceptions. Most important, nearly all of the states exempt non-profit organizations from the general prohibition. Other states do not require licensing, but still limit fees agencies can charge or other practices.[10]

There is a growing trend, particularly in states that are enacting new legislation in this area, to cover debt settlement agencies in their debt management laws. If the definitions in the state debt management law are sufficiently broad to cover debt settlement, the typical for-profit debt settlement agency will most likely be violating the law in numerous ways. Most clearly, the average debt settlement agency charges fees substantially higher than the fee limits in many state debt management laws.

A full list of the state debt management laws, including summaries of each law, can be found on the CD-Rom.

3. Unfair and Deceptive Acts and Practices (UDAP) Laws

Every state and the District of Columbia have enacted at least one statute broadly applicable to most consumer transactions. These laws are aimed at preventing consumer deception and abuses in the marketplace. NCLC's manual contains detailed information about these laws.

A threshold question is whether the state UDAP law applies to non-profit organizations. Again, this will be an issue of concern mainly in the credit counseling context. UDAP laws should

---

10. Ark. Code Ann. § 5-63-301 et seq.; Colo. Rev. Stat. Ann. § 12-14-103 (debt collector law explicitly exempts non-profit credit counselors); Del. Code Ann. tit. 11, § 910; Fla. Stat. Ann. § 817.801 through 817.806 (credit counseling), Fla. Stat. Ann. §559.10-559.13 (budget planners); Ga. Code Ann. § 18-5-1-18-5-4; Guam St. tit. 14, § 7101-7113; Haw. Rev. Stat. § 446-1-446-4; Ky. Rev. Stat. § 380.010-380.990; Mass. Gen. Laws ch. 180, § 4A; Mo. Rev. Stat. § 425.010-425.040; Mont. Code Ann. § 31-3-201-31-3-203; N.M. Stat. Ann. § 56-2-1-56-2-4; N.C. Gen. Stat. § 14-423-14-426; N.D. Cent. Code §§ 13-06-01 (definitions); 13-07-01-13-07-07; Okla. Stat. tit. 24, § 15 through 18; 18 Pa. Cons. Stat. § 7312; S.D. Codified Laws § 22-47-1-22-47-3; Tenn. Code Ann. § 39-14-142; Tex. Fin. Ann. Code § 394.101-394.103; Wash. Rev. Code § 18.28.010-18.28.190; W. Va. Code § 61-10-23; Wyo. Stat. Ann. § 33-14-101.

cover non-profit organizations because unlike the federal FTC Act, most state UDAP laws are not limited to acts by "corporations."[11] Even the relatively narrow scope of the FTC Act has been found to apply to nonprofit organizations to the extent they engage in business activities.[12]

Advocates should also carefully review their state UDAP laws to ensure that they apply even if the debt relief industry in question is arguably regulated or permitted by other laws.[13]

4. Other Consumer Protection and Common Law Claims

Unauthorized practice of law statutes and regulations[14] and state loan broker laws[15] may also apply. Unauthorized practice of law issues are particularly relevant against debt settlement companies. Many of these companies advise consumers about basic strategies to deal with debt collection and other collection tactics they may face while they are paying the debt settlement agency and not paying their creditors.

Common law claims such as fraud and breach of contract should also be considered.

5. Abuse of Non-Profit Status

The "non-profit exemption" in many consumer protection laws is especially problematic for advocates seeking to assist victims of unscrupulous credit counseling agencies. This is because the I.R.S. has granted non-profit status to many credit counseling agencies that are "for-profits in disguise."[16] The vast majority of credit counseling agencies are non-profit organizations. From 1994 through early 2004, 1215 credit counseling agencies applied to the I.R.S. for section 501(c)(3) tax-exempt status.[17] Over 800 of these agencies applied between 2000 and 2003.[18]

A key to improving regulation in this industry is for the I.R.S. and state regulators to aggressively enforce the standards for non-profit eligibility. There are promising signs that the I.R.S. is heading in this direction. First, in January 2003, the I.R.S. released a report signaling the agency's increased awareness of problems with credit counseling agencies.[19] Facing pressure throughout 2003, the I.R.S, along with the FTC and state regulators, issued a rare joint announcement in October 2003 advising consumers to beware of problems with certain credit counseling organizations.[20] Testifying in Congress in March 2004, I.R.S. Commissioner Mark Everson stated that his agency is examining the tax-exempt status of more than fifty credit counseling organizations.[21] The I.R.S. has since given some indications of the criteria it will use to assess whether a credit counseling agency merits non-profit status. Selected I.R.S. memoranda and reports related to credit counseling are available on the companion CD Rom.

11. See National Consumer Law Center, Unfair and Deceptive Acts and Practices § 2.3.5 (6th ed. 2004).
12. Id.
13. See Id. § 2.3.3.
14. See Id. § 5.12.2.4.
15. See Id. § 5.1.3.1.
16. Non-profit status is technically a state law concept, making an organization eligible for certain benefits, such as state sales, property, and income tax exemptions. Although most federal tax-exempt organizations are non-profit, organizing as a non-profit at the state level does not automatically grant the organization exemption from federal income tax. The terms "tax-exempt" and "non-profit" organizations or corporations are used interchangeably in this section even though there are some differences between them. For more information, see Internal Revenue Service, "Charities and Non-Profits", and I.R.S. Publication 557, Tax-Exempt Status for Your Organization, available at www.irs.gov.
17. U.S. Senate Permanent Subcommittee on Investigations, Committee on Governmental Affairs, Profiteering in a Non-Profit Industry: Abusive Practices in Credit Counseling (Mar. 24, 2004), available at http://govt-aff.senate.gov/_files/032404psistaffreport_creditcounsel.pdf (last visited December 2004).
18. Id.
19. Debra Cowen and Debra Kawecki, Credit Counseling Organizations, CPE 2004-1 (Jan. 9, 2003), available at www.irs.gov/pub/irs-tege/eotopica04.pdf (last visited December 2004).
20. FTC, IRS and State Regulators Urge Care When Seeking Help from Credit Counseling Organizations (Oct. 13, 2003), available at www.irs.gov/newsroom/article/0,,id=114574,00.html (last visited August 2004).
21. Senate Committee on Governmental Affairs, Profiteering in a Non-Profit Industry: Abusive Practices in Credit Counseling (Mar. 24, 2004) (statement of the Honorable Mark W. Everson), available at http://govt-aff.senate.gov/index.cfm? Fuseaction=Hearings.Testimony&HearingID=158&WitnessID=492.

Because of the I.R.S. efforts, it is important for advocates to send complaints about particular agencies to the I.R.S. as well as to the FTC and state consumer protection agencies.

III. ADDITIONAL CONSUMER PROTECTION LAWS

The laws discussed below may apply when suing abusive debt relief agencies, but also more generally to help consumers with debt problems. These critical laws are discussed very briefly in this section. Advocates seeking detailed information should consult the NCLC manuals.

1. Telemarketing

Telemarketing laws are relevant not only because many debt relief agencies violate these laws, but also to help protect consumers that are the victims of all types of telemarketing fraud.

In the debt relief industry, some non-profit agencies have teamed up with for-profit telemarketers to aggressively sell services to consumers. In some cases, these schemes are developed to evade the FTC do-not-call rules, which generally do not apply to non-profit organizations. Federal and state telemarketing laws may apply in cases against these agencies. A brief summary of these laws can be found below. More detailed information is available in NCLC's publication, Unfair and Deceptive Acts and Practices.

Telemarketing is covered by several different, sometimes overlapping federal and state statutes and regulations. Each of the following should be considered when evaluating complaints of telemarketing fraud.

The Telephone Consumer Protection Act (TCPA) is administered by the Federal Communications Commission.[22] The TCPA offers a private cause of action in state court for any violation. It focuses mostly on abusive methods of contacting the consumer, such as unsolicited faxes and prerecorded messages, but also restricts telephone solicitations at inconvenient hours.

The Telemarketing and Consumer Fraud and Abuse Prevention Act is administered by the Federal Trade Commission (FTC).[23] It offers a private cause of action but only where the plaintiff's damages exceed $50,000. This Act and the corresponding rules (Telemarketing Sales Rule)[24] focus on the content of telemarketing calls, forbidding various forms of deception and abuse. It overlaps with the Telephone Consumer Protection Act in its prohibition of calls at inconvenient hours.

Violations of telemarketing laws were key allegations in recent FTC actions against debt settlement companies. For example, the FTC sued National Consumer Council and related organizations in 2004, claiming violations of the Federal Trade Commission Act, the Telemarketing and Consumer Fraud and Abuse Prevention Act and the Gramm-Leach-Bliley Act.[25] The complaint describes an elaborate scheme fronted by a non-profit agency, National Consumer Council, which allegedly left voice message advertisements on consumers' home answering machines with the goal of generating clients for its affiliated debt negotiation programs.[26]

---

22. 47 U.S.C. § 227.
23. 15 U.S.C. § 6101-6108.
24. 16 C.F.R. Part 310.
25. FTC v. National Consumer Council, et seq., Case No. SACV-04-0474 CJC, available at http://www.ftc.gov/os/2004/05/040423 ncccomplaint.pdf. C.D. Ca., complaint filed April 23, 2004.
26. Id. See also National Consumer Law Center, Unfair and Deceptive Acts and Practices § 5.9.4.6 (6th ed. 2004) (telemarketing and "do not call" laws).

Information about practical steps to prevent or remedy telemarketing fraud is included on the CD-Rom.

2. Fair Debt Collection

Federal law and many states prohibit harassment by collection agencies (and in some states by creditors). The federal law can be found at 15 U.S.C. §1692 et seq. Most states also have fair debt laws. In many cases, the state laws provide additional protections. For example, the federal law applies only to third-party collectors. Some state laws have laws that govern creditors collecting their own debts.

Consumers have the right to be free from debt collection harassment regardless of whether they owe the underlying debt. Legal claims may be raised affirmatively or as counterclaims in collection suits. Sample pleadings are included in the companion CD Rom. For more information about fair debt laws and other ways to challenge debt collector harassment, see NCLC's manual *Fair Debt Collection* (5th ed. 2004). This manual contains an appendix with a summary of state debt collection laws.

There is some question whether fair debt laws cover credit counseling and other debt relief companies. Similar to the CROA discussed above, the federal fair debt law exempts certain non-profit organizations. Only those non-profit organizations which at the request of consumers perform bona fide consumer credit counseling and assist consumers in the liquidation of their debts by receiving payments from such consumers and distributing such amounts to creditors are exempt.[27]

One court that addressed this issue agreed that the distinction between credit counseling and debt collection is finely cut, but that the FDCPA did not apply.[28] The court found that credit counseling agencies are not debt collectors as they do not collect debts owed to others; rather, they assume such debts as part of their method, whatever its merits, of credit counseling.[29]

In other cases, the law should apply as long as the other threshold definitional requirements are met. Most important, the agency must be shown to be regularly collecting debts owed to another party.

3. Fair Credit Reporting Act

The federal Fair Credit Reporting Act and state analogues provide consumers with a number of basic rights including:

- Rules about who can review a consumer credit report;

- Time limits for reporting of negative credit information;

- Procedures for fixing errors in credit reports; and

- Private remedies for violations of certain sections of the law.

---

27. 15 U.S.C. §1692a(6)(E).
28. Limpert v. Cambridge Credit Counseling, 328 F. Supp. 2d 360 (E.D.N.Y. 2004)
29. Id.

The federal law can be found at 15 U.S.C. §1681 et seq.

This law and similar state laws are discussed in detail in NCLC's manual *Fair Credit Reporting*.

4. Fair Credit Billing Rights

Basic consumer rights to challenge errors in credit card billing are discussed in Chapter 4 of this workbook. Consumers rights to challenge billing errors can be found at 15 U.S.C. § 1666. There are also separate requirements in the Truth in Lending Act that allow consumers to raise claims or defenses against credit card issuers. See 15 U.S.C. § 1666i. Consumer education information about credit cards is included on the companion CD-Rom.

These issues are covered in a number of NCLC publications, including *Truth in Lending* and *Consumer Banking and Payments Law*.

5. Credit Discrimination Laws

Two main federal laws, the Equal Credit Opportunity Act (ECOA), 15 U.S.C. §§ 1691-1691f, and the Fair Housing Act (FHA), 42 U.S.C. §§ 3601-3631 cover most credit discrimination situations. The ECOA prohibits discrimination in any part of a credit transaction, including applications for credit, credit evaluation, credit terms and even collection procedures.

To help borrowers figure out if a creditor is making a decision based on discrimination, the ECOA requires creditors to give notice when they deny credit applications or change the terms. If they deny a credit application, they must give a written explanation of the reasons for the denial.

Not all types of discrimination are illegal. The ECOA prohibits a creditor from discriminating based on these factors:

- Race or color;
- National origin;
- Sex;
- Marital status;
- Religion;
- Age; or
- Public Assistance Status.

The ECOA also prohibits creditors from discriminating against consumers for exercising their rights under consumer protection laws.

The federal Fair Housing Act (FHA) prohibits discrimination in residential real estate transactions. The law protects consumers from discrimination not only in the rental housing market but also in the home mortgage market. The FHA, like the ECOA, prohibits discrimination based on race, color, religion, national origin, and sex. In addition, the FHA covers discrimination based on familial status and disability.

A few states have laws that prohibit credit discrimination on grounds other than those covered by the ECOA and FHA. For example, some states prohibit credit discrimination based on sexual orientation. Information about these state laws as well as detailed information about the federal laws can be found in NCLC's publication, Credit Discrimination.

ORDER FORM

QTY:

_____ **The NCLC Guide to Surviving Debt** (2005 ed.) (422 pages) . . . . . .$19 ppd.
(SAVE! $14 each for 5 or more, $12 for 20 or more, $8 for 100 or more.)

_____ **The NCLC Guide to Consumer Rights for Immigrants** (2002 ed.)
(100 pages) . . . .$10 ppd.

_____ **The NCLC Guide to Mobile Homes** (2002 ed.) (134 pages) . . . . . .$12 ppd.

_____ **Return to Sender: Getting a Refund or Replacement for
Your Lemon Car** (2000 ed.) (192 pages) . . . .$16 ppd.

❏ **Please send me more information about NCLC books for lawyers.**

Name _____

Organization _____

Street Address _____

City _____ State _____ Zip _____

Telephone _____ Fax _____

E-mail _____

MAIL TO: National Consumer Law Center, Inc.
Publications Department
77 Summer Street, 10th Floor
Boston, MA 02110-1006

❏ **Check or money order enclosed, payable to the National Consumer Law Center**

AMERICAN EXPRESS **VISA** **MasterCard** Card# _____ Exp. date _____

Signature _____
(card number, expiration date, and signature must accompany charge orders)

NATIONAL CONSUMER LAW CENTER
77 Summer Street, 10th Floor ▪ Boston, MA 02110-1006
Tel. (617) 542-9595 ▪ FAX (617) 542-8028 ▪ publications@nclc.org
Telephone orders (617) 542-9595 ▪ or fax (617) 542-8028 for credit card orders

ABOUT THE COMPANION CD-ROM

The *Surviving Credit Card Debt Workbook* companion CD-Rom contains a wealth of material for consumers and their advocates, including references, consumer organization and government reports, and documents that can be easily adapted for personal use.

System Requirements
Use of this CD-Rom requires a Windows PC and Adobe Acrobat Reader. Acrobat Reader versions 5 and 6.0.1 are included free on this CD-Rom. Users of Windows 95 and Windows 98 First Edition must use Acrobat Reader 5; all other users are recommended to use Acrobat Reader 6.0.1. If you have Acrobat Reader 6.0, we **highly** recommend you install version 6.0.1 because of a troublesome bug in version 6.0.

Using the CD-Rom
To use the CD-Rom, simply insert it into your CD-Rom drive. After a few seconds, a pop-up menu will appear.*

If you do not already have Acrobat Reader 5 or 6.0.1 as discussed above, first click the **Install Acrobat Reader** button in the pop-up window. We strongly recommend that new Acrobat users read the Acrobat tutorial found in the main menu.

Once Acrobat Reader is installed—or if you already had it—click the **Start NCLC CD** button on the pop-up menu.

Acrobat documents are connected like web pages, with links and buttons you can click to navigate the menus and documents on the CD-Rom. The files also have bookmarks on the left side of the screen, which you can click to move within the current document or return to the main menu.

Selected documents are also available in Microsoft Word format to be more easily adapted for individual use. (Any current version of Word or WordPerfect can be used to open and edit these files.) Such material includes sample letters and certain legal documents for advocates such as pleadings and practice aids. The simplest way to find these materials is to locate and open the desired document using the menus in Acrobat Reader, and then click the "Word version" bookmark on the left. Your word processor will start and open the document automatically.

* If the pop-up menu doesn't open automatically, or if you have any other problems using the CD-Rom, see the Read_me.txt file.

IMPORTANT INFORMATION BEFORE OPENING THE CD-ROM PACKAGE